AMBITION FACING WEST

Anthony Clarvoe

I0139560

BROADWAY PLAY PUBLISHING INC
New York
www.broadwayplaypublishing.com
info@broadwayplaypublishing.com

AMBITION FACING WEST
© Copyright 2003 by Anthony Clarvoe

First published by B P P I : May 2003
First printing, this edition: October 2007
I S B N: 978-0-88145-368-3

Book design: Marie Donovan
Word processing: Microsoft Word for Windows
Typographic controls: Xerox Ventura Publisher 2.0 P E
Typeface: Palatino

ACKNOWLEDGMENTS

At a time when the Balkans were disturbing the world yet again, AMBITION FACING WEST began as an idea about my family's itinerary from that place through the twentieth century. Many people and organizations contributed their history, memory, and gifts to the play's creation. The first to respond with support were Oskar Eustis and the Center Theater Group/Mark Taper Forum, the John Simon Guggenheim Foundation, the McKnight Foundation, the Playwrights' Center, and the Immigration History Research Center at the University of Minnesota. The New Harmony Project gave me the chance to make it a play. Workshops at Cleveland Playhouse and the Mark Taper Forum took it further. It was a particular pleasure that the first production was directed by Oskar Eustis at Trinity Rep, years after our first conversations. Intiman Theater and Repertory Theater of St Louis followed with generous productions. The Bloomsburg Theater Ensemble gave me the chance to act on what I'd learned from those productions and write this draft for them.

For their hospitality to me and the play in all our travels, my particular thanks to Janet Allen, Melia Bensussen, Tom Bryant, The Chase Fund, Katherine Heasley Clarvoe, William Craver, Gordon Davidson, Frank Dwyer, Liz Engleman, Oskar Eustis, Kip Gould, Susan Gregg, Peter Hackett, James Houghton, Laurie McCants, Mark Ramont, Warner Shook, and Steve Woolf. Thanks too to the many artists and audiences who shared their own families' journeys and saw their reflection in this one.

This play is dedicated to Erna Radalj Clarvoe.

The world premiere of AMBITION FACING WEST was presented by Trinity Repertory Company, Oskar Eustis, Artistic Director, Patricia Egan, Managing Director, on 18 April 1997. The cast and creative contributors were:

YOUNG STIPAN/JIM/JOEY .... Mauro Hantman
FATHER LUKA .... William Damkoehler
MISS ADAMIC/YOUNG ALMA .... Elizabeth Quincy
MARIJA/ALMA .... Anne Scurria
IVO/STIPAN .... Timothy Crowe
MRS ADAMIC/JOSEPHINA .... Phyllis Kay

Director .... Oskar Eustis
Set .... Christine Jones
Lighting .... Geoff Korf
Costumes .... William Lane
Stage manager .... Cole Bonenberger

The premiere of this version of AMBITION FACING
WEST was presented on 21 January 2000 by the
Bloomsburg Theater Ensemble. The cast and creative
contributors were:

YOUNG STIPAN/JIM .... David Snider
FATHER LUKA/EUGENE .... Peter Brown
MARIJA/ALMA .... Elizabeth Dowd
IVO/STIPAN .... Michael Collins
MISS ADAMIC/YOUNG ALMA .... Nina Czitrom
MRS ADAMIC/JOSEPHINA .... Laurie McCants
JOEY .... Pete Rush

Director .... Mark Ramont
Set .... Eric Renschler
Lighting .... A C Hickox
Costumes .... Lora Dole
Sound .... Whit MacLaughlin
Stage manager .... Frankie Ocasio

PLACES, TIMES & CHARACTERS

Croatia, 1910:

YOUNG STIPAN
FATHER LUKA
MARIJA, STIPAN's *mother*
IVO, *the Amerikanac*
MISS ADAMIC
MRS ADAMIC

Wyoming, 1940s:

YOUNG ALMA
JOSEPHINA, ALMA's *mother*
STIPAN, ALMA's *father*
JIM

Japan, 1980s:

ALMA
JOEY, ALMA's *son*
EUGENE

Stage: Gravel. Something like water. Wood planking. Sky.

ACT ONE

(Croatia, 1910)

(MISS ADAMIC, in a sailor-style dress and pinafore, kneels, guiding a model sailboat with a long wand. At a distance from her, FATHER LUKA and YOUNG STIPAN are sitting in the sun sparkling off the water. MARIJA stands, fists on hips, baskets at her feet, watching YOUNG STIPAN. FATHER LUKA wears a cassock; YOUNG STIPAN and MARIJA wear peasant clothing. YOUNG STIPAN is holding a book. He is stealing glances at the girl as he reads aloud.)

YOUNG STIPAN: "And wonderfully among them all..."

FATHER LUKA: The infinitive is "to shine."

YOUNG STIPAN: "...shone the son of Aeson for beauty and grace..."

FATHER LUKA: Good.

YOUNG STIPAN: "And the maiden looked at him with..." "Secret?" No.

FATHER LUKA: Stealthy, perhaps.

YOUNG STIPAN: "With stealthy glance, holding her bright..."

FATHER LUKA: Veil.

YOUNG STIPAN: "Holding her bright veil aside, her heart...smoldering with pain."

FATHER LUKA: Oh, very good.

YOUNG STIPAN: "And her soul creeping like a dream..."

FATHER LUKA: Flitted.

YOUNG STIPAN: "Flitted after him as he went. So they passed forth from the palace sorely troubled. And the maiden, Medea by name, followed, and much she brooded in her soul on all the cares that Love awakens."

MARIJA: Tell me again what this is good for.

FATHER LUKA: Well. It's a very old story.

MARIJA: I know all the old stories, I've told him stories. Sundays he hears the Gospels from you.

FATHER LUKA: This is a different old story. And he will be able to read it for himself.

MARIJA: Sounds Protestant. I have eggs to sell. (*She picks up her baskets. To* STIPAN) Don't make me have to come find you. (*She goes.*)

FATHER LUKA: You've been working.

YOUNG STIPAN: Thank you for the candle-ends, they helped. Will it get more exciting again?

FATHER LUKA: It depends on what you mean by exciting. Two pages on, you get Medea in her bedchamber, tormented by the pangs of love as is the waiting bride, entirely inappropriate for a boy your age. Where did we leave off?

(IVO *enters, carrying a valise, wearing a vested suit. He joins* YOUNG STIPAN *in gazing across at the girl.*)

IVO: (*A murmur*) A *villé*.

(FATHER LUKA *glances up appreciatively.*)

IVO: Yes? Look. (*Nodding toward the girl*) A *villé*.

FATHER LUKA: How apt, sir. I thought the belief had gone from memory.

IVO: Not from mine.

FATHER LUKA: I am quite the amateur collector of such folk tales.

IVO: *(Regarding the girl)* Ship owner's daughter?

FATHER LUKA: Mm.

IVO: When I was a boy, the ship owners were gods: like us, but much larger, and perfectly formed. They never died. Same name on the manifests, decade after decade. Ivo Pasic. A pleasure to meet you, Father.

(IVO and FATHER LUKA nod formally to each other.)

FATHER LUKA: Welcome home.

YOUNG STIPAN: Sir? You are *Amerikanac*?

IVO: Left the farm when I was about your age. *(Holding out a hand to YOUNG STIPAN)* Ivo Pasic. How do you do.

(YOUNG STIPAN, confused, does not move.)

IVO: It is the way Americans greet someone new. You take my hand, and we shake them. Up and down.

FATHER LUKA: Why is that?

IVO: I believe it is supposed to mean we have no weapons.

(IVO and YOUNG STIPAN shake hands.)

IVO: And then we say our names.

YOUNG STIPAN: I am Stipan.

IVO: Ivo Pasic.

FATHER LUKA: Mister Pasic. The *villé*? Please. Whatever you remember?

IVO: Once upon a time, the old people would say, when the world was a better place than it is today, if a young girl like that one died—God forbid—of a broken heart, she would become a *villé*.

FATHER LUKA: *(To* YOUNG STIPAN*)* Think of the nymphs of the classical texts.

IVO: They would live on for years—forever, some people said—in the woods and lakes near our village.

FATHER LUKA: So the *villé* lived with the living in friendship.

IVO: When shepherds fell asleep, *villé* watched their sheep and cattle.

FATHER LUKA: Pure, beautiful spirits.

IVO: Farm boys would see them at night in the fields, dancing and chanting, urging the crops to grow tall and thick.

FATHER LUKA: Hm.

(Each man finds himself looking over at MISS ADAMIC. MRS ADAMIC *enters, grandly dressed for a stroll in town, and crosses to* MISS ADAMIC. MRS ADAMIC *coolly eyes the three men as they stare at her daughter.)*

FATHER LUKA: Ah.

*(*STIPAN *looks away,* IVO *touches the brim of his hat decorously,* FATHER LUKA *raises two fingers in blessing.* MRS ADAMIC *taps her daughter on the shoulder.* MISS ADAMIC *stands and courtesies, shooting a glance at* YOUNG STIPAN *as she does. She starts hauling in her boat.)*

IVO: And no one believes in the *villé* anymore?

FATHER LUKA: Well, with so much war and evil in our land, the nymphs show themselves less often. I think they drift over the old villages, sad young spirits dressed in breeze and moonlight, tending to the newly dead, helping their souls to free themselves, helping them repair the wrongs they committed in the flesh.

IVO: Mm.

(A church bell rings. YOUNG STIPAN *jumps up. The women exit.)*

FATHER LUKA: I have confessions to hear. *(To* YOUNG STIPAN*)* I expect to hear yours after you get through that next passage about Medea. *(To* IVO*)* You will be with us a while?

IVO: I think so.

FATHER LUKA: I would love to talk again. *(To* YOUNG STIPAN*)* Run home before you're missed.

*(*FATHER LUKA *exits.* YOUNG STIPAN *bows quickly and starts to go.* IVO *holds up the book.)*

IVO: Your book.

*(*YOUNG STIPAN *turns back.)*

IVO: You have a boat?

*(*YOUNG STIPAN *nods.)*

IVO: Do boys still sail into the Bay of Viganj?

*(*YOUNG STIPAN *nods. He holds out his hand for his book.* IVO *keeps holding it.)*

IVO: You still drop hooks overboard? Cook fish on the rocks on the beach? Use shark skin for sandpaper?

*(*YOUNG STIPAN *nods.)*

IVO: Would your father beat you if he knew you were learning to read?

(Beat. YOUNG STIPAN *nods.)*

IVO: *The Argonautica.* Unusual text. *(He holds out the book.)*

YOUNG STIPAN: Father Luka says that Jason and the Argonauts sailed through here. On their way to the Golden Fleece.

(A foghorn sounds.)

IVO: Go.

(The lights crossfade to:)

(Wyoming, 1940s)

(Static. YOUNG ALMA and JOSEPHINA are sitting on kitchen chairs. YOUNG ALMA is fiddling with a crystal radio set with a battery and a speaker. JOSEPHINA is wearing a bed jacket and has braces on her legs. She crochets. Metal crutches lean on the back of her chair. A couple of books are on the floor. From the radio, a foghorn.)

RADIO ANNOUNCER: Out of the fog...
Out of the night...
And into his American adventures comes...
Bulldog Drummond!

(Static again. YOUNG ALMA growls and fiddles with the tuner.)

JOSEPHINA: What is happening?

YOUNG ALMA: I should be able to pull in Chicago....

(Staticky voices, then gunfire)

JOSEPHINA: Yes, that is Chicago.

(Shouts, police whistles, more shots)

JOSEPHINA: Your father did not bring you that radio kit all the way from Washington, DC so you could listen to stupid noise!

(YOUNG ALMA turns off the radio.)

YOUNG ALMA: I just thought... Everybody else has had them forever, and I know we can't afford a real one, but... I thought if I built this myself... I thought I could give you music.

JOSEPHINA: Is the supper ready for your Papa?

YOUNG ALMA: Supper is ready, his shirts are ironed, everything's done.

JOSEPHINA: You do not like all the chores, I know—

YOUNG ALMA: It's fine.

JOSEPHINA: I wish *my* Mama was there to give me this teaching. I am making you ready for your life.

YOUNG ALMA: I know.

JOSEPHINA: You want to read to me?

(YOUNG ALMA *picks up a book.*)

YOUNG ALMA: Starting a new one today.

JOSEPHINA: Story book?

YOUNG ALMA: American story book. *(Turning pages)* Contents, notes... Chapter One. *(Looking up)* How old were you when you and Papa got married?

JOSEPHINA: Too young. Why.

YOUNG ALMA: Just curious.

JOSEPHINA: Is this about that Jim?

YOUNG ALMA: Just curious.

JOSEPHINA: Nobody is just curious. Curious wants something. Are you thinking about getting married with that Jim?

YOUNG ALMA: Thinking about it. Not planning on it.

JOSEPHINA: Is there a reason to hurry the thinking?

YOUNG ALMA: What do you mean?

JOSEPHINA: Just curious. Chapter One.

YOUNG ALMA: Chapter One. *(Reading)* "You don't know about me, without you have read a book by the name of *The Adventures of Tom Sawyer*, but that ain't no matter."

(Japan, 1980s)

(Lights up on JOEY, *eighties coastal casual. Discman, RayBans, Gameboy, cell phone, all at once. He vibrates.)*

YOUNG ALMA: *(Reading)* "That book was made by Mr Mark Twain, and he told the truth, mainly..."

*(*ALMA *enters, in an eighties business suit, talking on her cell phone and smoking a cigarette. As she speaks, the lights fade on* YOUNG ALMA *and* JOSEPHINA.*)*

ALMA: *(Into phone, loudly)* Where are you? Man, every time the home office flies people over, guess who gets to show 'em the sights? Take a lot of Type A types to the shrines of Zen Buddhism, makes total sense to me. They have this gravel pit out back, I came out to sneak a cigarette. This connection is terrible, where are you, a tool and die works?

*(*JOEY *pulls the Walkman earphone from his ear and holds it to the mouthpiece of his cell phone.* ALMA *recoils from her cell phone.)*

ALMA: Ow!

JOEY: *(Holding up a hand)* Hey, Mom.

ALMA: Smidgen! You made it!

(She starts toward him. He continues to speak to her through the phone.)

JOEY: Oh, hey, Mother?

ALMA: *(Stopping)* What did I do?

JOEY: It's not a gravel pit.

ALMA: *(Looking out)* It isn't?

JOEY: It's the monastery garden.

ALMA: It's rocks.

JOEY: It's a rock garden.

ALMA: Good, that's a good thing. Easy to maintain. *(Staring)* It reminds me of the Sheraton Atlanta, why is that?

(JOEY *shrugs.*)

ALMA: We could hang up.

JOEY: Don't yet? You sound more like you this way.

(Beat)

ALMA: Hey, remember when I was traveling, I'd read you bedtime stories on the phone?

JOEY: Mm. Where The Wild Things Are.

ALMA: Sure.

JOEY: Wind In The Willows. The Hobbit, Lord of the Rings —

ALMA: Sure...

JOEY: The Complete Works of Charles Dickens, *Remembrance of Things Past—*

ALMA: *Okay.*

(Beat. She puts away her phone.)

JOEY: Huckleberry Finn.

ALMA: Yeah. *(Beat)* How was it in the States?

JOEY: *(Putting away his phone)* It was okay.

ALMA: Okay? That's it?

JOEY: Yeah.

ALMA: Oh, Smidgen, I'm sorry.

(He shrugs.)

JOEY: Guess I kind of built it up in my mind.

ALMA: Streets were just paved with pavement, huh?

JOEY: I thought, America, you know, I'll go there, it'll be home. I'll feel at home.

ALMA: No?

JOEY: Everybody's talking about the eighties, "It's the eighties," like a decade is a new place where anything you do is okay, hey no problem it's the eighties, we're in the morality-free zone.

(He is moving to the music and playing his game. ALMA *watches.*

ALMA: How can you hold a conversation?

JOEY: I'm multi-tasking.

ALMA: You're not-any-tasking.

(He shrugs.)

ALMA: You want to be here? You're just in time. War's breaking out.

(Off his look)

ALMA: Trade war.

JOEY: Which side are we on?

ALMA: Our side.

(He shrugs.)

JOEY: Cool.

ALMA: You shrug a lot.

JOEY: Yeah?

ALMA: It's a tic you've got.

JOEY: Don't do the posture thing.

ALMA: What posture thing.

JOEY: Where you comment on my shoulders and pull them back so I'll be standing up straight. It's a tic you've got.

ALMA: Thank you for telling me, I had no idea,
I'll never let it happen again.

JOEY: Mother. If it were a problem I wouldn't have
brought it up.

(She takes out a cigarette and a Zippo lighter.)

ALMA: I wish you could warn me before the difficult
conversations. Now I need another cigarette. *(Looking
at him)* Turn that damn thing off!

(He does. He looks at her. She looks away.)

RADIO ANNOUNCER: Who knows what evil lurks in the
hearts of men?

(Lights up on YOUNG ALMA and JOSEPHINA.)

JOSEPHINA: *(Standing)* Alma!

JOEY: Mom?

RADIO ANNOUNCER: The Shadow knows....

JOSEPHINA: *(As she goes)* Your father does not bring you
that radio kit all the way from Washington, D C—

(ALMA and YOUNG ALMA join her, quietly:)

JOSEPHINA, ALMA & YOUNG ALMA: —just so you could
listen to stupid noise!

*(YOUNG ALMA and ALMA growl softly. YOUNG ALMA
fiddles with the radio silently.)*

ALMA: *(To JOEY)* This couldn't be about your Dad?

JOEY: No.

ALMA: No, of course not—

JOEY: I dream about him sometimes.

ALMA: —I'm here, so I'm the one—you have dreams
about him?

JOEY: Sometimes.

ALMA: Do you even remember a face?

JOEY: There's a face. I feel myself calling it "Dad."

ALMA: What happens.

JOEY: Dreams are boring.

ALMA: Not yours.

JOEY: Besides, they're not like dreams, anyway.
They're kind of just real.

(YOUNG ALMA *turns a knob on the radio. A distant
orchestra plays the Barcarole from Offenbach's* Les
Contes d'Hoffmann.)

YOUNG ALMA: *(Calling)* Better, Mama?

JOSEPHINA: *(Calling, off)* Better if it was Verdi!

YOUNG ALMA: *(Calling)* The Verdi isn't till Saturday.
(She pages through her book as she exits.)

JOEY: It's evening.

(Sunset slowly fills the stage.)

JOEY: We're walking by the ocean.

ALMA: Am I there?

JOEY: Sometimes.

ALMA: We did that. Walked by the Pacific.
Swinging you between us.

JOEY: Sometimes not.

ALMA: But... Okay.

JOEY: Sometimes that's it. But sometimes washed
up on shore there's a boat.

(Croatia, 1910)

(IVO *and* YOUNG STIPAN *enter, pushing a rowboat.)*

ALMA: *(To* JOEY*)* A boat?

JOEY: And he says, "Come on."

(As JOEY *speaks,* IVO *and* YOUNG STIPAN *get into the boat.)*

JOEY: Sometimes he helps me in. Sometimes I help him. He rolls up his pantlegs and climbs inside and I roll up my pantlegs and push the prow till the sand lets go and he's floating and I climb in. And we row.

ALMA: And that's how it starts.

JOEY: Sometimes.

IVO: The moment I sailed my little boat into the Bay of Viganj, I was happy.

*(*IVO *settles in.* YOUNG STIPAN *rows.)*

IVO: So quiet I could hear the shellfish below me, opening and closing. I'd lean over the side and watch the fish hunting for food, or I'd lean back and watch the clouds sailing away on the western wind. What kind of marker, did he say?

YOUNG STIPAN: A little orange float.

IVO: Croatia never changes. Boys farm by day and smuggle by night. You're a smart boy. Taking the *Amerikanac* for a sentimental ride in the moonlight, yes? I'm your cover. *(Pointing downward)* Look!

YOUNG STIPAN: The marker?

IVO: No. Even by moonlight, after so long, still clear, right to the bottom. An earthquake made all this, piled up all those big stones. I used to imagine I was looking at some dead city, with white sand glimmering in the streets.

YOUNG STIPAN: *(Looking)* Is that what a city looks like?

IVO: If you could float above it and see it.

YOUNG STIPAN: Like a *villé.*

IVO: Like a *villé.*

(The music has faded to silence.)

YOUNG STIPAN: Sir? Why did you leave?

IVO: Do you know Marco Polo was from here?

YOUNG STIPAN: I thought he was Italian.

IVO: He was. His father was here during the Venetian occupation.

YOUNG STIPAN: Goddamn Venetians.

IVO: Heroes come from this place. I think I see the marker.

YOUNG STIPAN: Yes. *(He mans the oars again.)*

IVO: What is it?

YOUNG STIPAN: A casque of cigars and whiskey, the captain said.

IVO: You can do the hauling.

*(*YOUNG STIPAN *rows.)*

ALMA: *(To* JOEY*)* And you're happy in these dreams.

JOEY: Yes.

ALMA: You and your old man, heading for adventure.

JOEY: No. We don't head anywhere. We row to the horizon. And then we sit. Dad ships the oars. We just sit. Rocking. Ready to start. But not quite yet.

YOUNG STIPAN: *(To* IVO*)* What is it like in America?

IVO: Why do you ask? *(Beat)* American boys, all they do is go to school and play.

YOUNG STIPAN: Cowboys and Indians. Have you seen any? Real ones?

IVO: No, the cowboys killed off the Indians, then a lot of German farmers came and killed off the cowboys. Now

their children play cowboys and Indians. Do you know
what else they play?

YOUNG STIPAN: What?

IVO: Pirates. They pretend they're out sailing in boats,
hauling in treasure.

YOUNG STIPAN: But—

IVO: Stipan. Somewhere in America, a child is dreaming
he is you.

(YOUNG ALMA *enters slowly, reading from her book. She
carries a bowl.*)

YOUNG ALMA: "I never felt easy till the raft was out in
the middle of the Mississippi."

IVO: And you dream to be that American. Don't you,
Stipan.

(YOUNG ALMA *sits. As she reads, she snaps the peas in the
bowl.*)

YOUNG ALMA: *(Reading)* "I was powerful glad to get
away from the feuds, and so was Jim to get away from
the swamp. We said there warn't no home like a raft,
after all."

IVO: Always been the same. Marco Polo and his father.
Jason and Herakles. A boy and a man on a boat.

YOUNG ALMA: *(Reading)* "Other places do seem so
cramped up and smothery, but a raft don't."

IVO: A boy and a man on a boat. This is how the
American dreams he is free.

YOUNG STIPAN: But the American is free already,
isn't he?

IVO: The thing about free is that nobody knows when
he is.

JOEY: Sometimes Dad says, "Ready?" and I say, "Ready," and he dips the oars. I always wake up then. And it's morning. The dream, when I have it, it's always my last one before the day starts.

ALMA: In real life he never took you anywhere alone.

JOEY: I *know.*

ALMA: *I* did that stuff.

JOEY: Or you read to me about it.

(ALMA looks at her younger self.)

YOUNG ALMA: *(Reading)* "You feel mighty free and easy and comfortable, on a raft." *(She continues snapping peas.)*

YOUNG STIPAN: *(To* IVO*)* Everything I want to do here, there's already a reason I can't.

IVO: What are they, these things you want so badly to do?

YOUNG STIPAN: I don't know. I'd be happy just to be in a place where it's all right to want something. I'd worry about *what* I want when I got there.

IVO: Freedom. Yes, I know just the place.

JOEY: *(To* ALMA*)* Listen. Are there jobs here?

ALMA: The joint is jumpin'.

JOEY: There's nothing in the States.

ALMA: An American boy who's lived in Japan? The world's got plans for you, kiddo. What are you looking for?

JOEY: Whatever. Anything.

ALMA: But...

JOEY: What.

IVO: *(To* YOUNG STIPAN*)* Do you know what I dream to be? Of anything in the world?

YOUNG STIPAN: What?

IVO: You.

YOUNG STIPAN: *What?*

ALMA: *(To* JOEY*)* What are you looking to do, though?

JOEY: Beats me. Advance me enough for a suit, I'll be Joey the Saririman, I don't care.

ALMA: You're supposed to care.

JOEY: I won't make you look bad. You know me, I'll work like a dog.

ALMA: It's not that. It's your life, Joey.

JOEY: I know.

ALMA: Don't you care what happens to it?

JOEY: Sure. Absolutely.

*(*JOEY *plays with his Gameboy.* ALMA *looks at him.)*

YOUNG STIPAN: *(To* IVO*)* You've seen everything, been all over, me—

IVO: I used to be you, once. In the last century. But if I were you, now, I could look forward to being a man in America. With everything about to happen, new century gotten a good running start, wife and a house full of children around me, in a world of peace. I'd give my soul, God help me but I would. Take me with you, Stipan.

YOUNG STIPAN: But—

IVO: Pack my soul, let me slip in your ear for safekeeping, carry me with you in your eyes. Let me be you, Stipan, a generation from now, in beautiful America.

(As YOUNG ALMA *reads,* YOUNG STIPAN *gets out and steadies the boat for* IVO*.)*

YOUNG ALMA: *(Reading)* "It's lovely to live on a raft."
(She gently swirls her bowl of peas and smiles at a thought.)
"We had the sky, up there, all speckled with stars,
and we used to lay on our backs and look up at them,
and discuss about whether they was made, or only just
happened..."

*(IVO steps out of the boat, IVO no longer. He carries a
suitcase and a folded newspaper. He crosses toward YOUNG
ALMA, entering—)*

(Wyoming, 1940s)

(YOUNG ALMA looks up.)

YOUNG ALMA: Papa!

JOSEPHINA: *(Calling, off)* Stipan?

YOUNG ALMA: Welcome home.

(YOUNG ALMA closes the book. Everyone else goes.)

STIPAN: Is there a wind?

YOUNG ALMA: Not yet.

STIPAN: Goddamn Wyoming. *(Fanning himself with the
newspaper)* Got to do everything yourself.

(He exits. YOUNG ALMA snaps peas.)

JOSEPHINA: *(Off; calling reproachfully)* Stipan!

*(STIPAN reenters, carrying the folded newspaper and
dragging a kitchen chair. He has taken off his jacket of his
creased but sturdy three-piece summer business suit.)*

STIPAN: *(Calling)* It will be cooler out here, *cara!*
Do you need us?

JOSEPHINA: *(Calling)* I am okay!

(STIPAN sits and fans himself for a beat.)

YOUNG ALMA: You look tired, Papa.

STIPAN: No business being tired, all I did all day was sit on the train.

YOUNG ALMA: It's hard work sitting in the heat like that for hours.

STIPAN: *(Calling)* You hear that, *cara*? We *are* Americans, I'm going to tell them the next time they yell at me in the street, I'll say, I am an American, I can prove it by my daughter, she thinks that sitting in the heat doing nothing is a hard day's work. In the old country, that was the sabbath.

YOUNG ALMA: Who yells at you in the street?

STIPAN: Nobody. And they are stupid. They don't even get their insults right, they think I am Italian, they sing, "Mussolini...!" What is a weenie?

(Beat)

YOUNG ALMA: It's a word for sausage, on a roll.

STIPAN: The hot dog.

YOUNG ALMA: The hot dog. Why?

STIPAN: The hot dog—is this also called a fire dog?

YOUNG ALMA: I don't think so, why?

STIPAN: One time I turned to the shouting man and his friends, and I said, "You are wrong, I am no Italian, I am a Dalmatian." They laughed at this very much.

(Beat)

YOUNG ALMA: And they called you a fire dog. You.

STIPAN: Can you explain this?

YOUNG ALMA: No. No. *(Beat)* Did you see the ocean?

STIPAN: Mm.

YOUNG ALMA: How was it?

STIPAN: Still the same.

YOUNG ALMA: What is it like?

STIPAN: Never still.

(JOSEPHINA *enters, using her crutches.*)

JOSEPHINA: What do you care about the ocean?
Have you ever seen an ocean?

YOUNG ALMA: No, Mama.

JOSEPHINA: So. (JOSEPHINA *sits. During the following
she and* YOUNG ALMA *perform* JOSEPHINA's *routine of
physical therapy exercises.*)

YOUNG ALMA: In science class Mrs. Tonovich says they
think all of Wyoming used to be at the bottom of the
ocean.

STIPAN: May history repeat itself.

YOUNG ALMA: A warm, shallow, tropical sea. Teeming
with life.

JOSEPHINA: Stipan, she is talking about the Flood, yes?
Noah and the Ark.

YOUNG ALMA: And the earth pushed Wyoming up out
of the ocean, up into the air, like a long, slow
earthquake.

JOSEPHINA: And here we are, high and dry. *Se dice cosi*?

STIPAN: *Si.*

JOSEPHINA: That is what happens.

YOUNG ALMA: I like to think of Papa on the ocean.
On a boat.

(*Lights up on* YOUNG STIPAN, *coiling a line with an orange
float on one end. He stares into the distance.* STIPAN *looks at
him.*)

STIPAN: You've never seen the ocean.

YOUNG ALMA: Only pictures.

STIPAN: See, that's no good. You have to see for yourself. The ocean moves, that's the point about the ocean.

YOUNG ALMA: What does it feel like on a boat?

JOSEPHINA: Boats. We come over on boats. I am happy forever I am as far from boats as a person can be.

YOUNG ALMA: Hush, Mama. Work, now. *(As they work)* Do you miss it, Papa? The ocean? Is that why you went to see it?

STIPAN: No.

(Lights down on YOUNG STIPAN. STIPAN *turns to his family.)*

STIPAN: No, a senator made us come all the way out to his yacht to remind us the coal miners would be not patriotic to strike.

JOSEPHINA: Stupid.*(To* YOUNG ALMA*) Basta, basta.*

STIPAN: Very stupid. Away from that Washington, though, talking was more possible. He even listened a little. Things seem more possible on the water. It's bigger than the sky here.

YOUNG ALMA: Is that possible?

STIPAN: Oh, you Great Plain people and your big sky. Why isn't it possible?

YOUNG ALMA: Well, Papa, the ocean we can see is limited by the curvature of the earth, but the sky—

JOSEPHINA: You two don't talk too late.

(With their help, JOSEPHINA *stands.)*

YOUNG ALMA: I'll come in a minute.

*(*JOSEPHINA *goes, slowly.)*

STIPAN: What about the sky?

YOUNG ALMA: Here, I'll draw. *(She draws in the gravel as she talks.)* Here's the earth. And here's us, standing up on it. I'm exaggerating the scale of course.

STIPAN: Of course.

(JOSEPHINA turns and watches them for a moment before she goes.)

YOUNG ALMA: We draw a straight line—light doesn't curve under normal physical conditions—from our eyes. It makes a tangent with the circle of the earth. Now imagine this circle is a globe and you can draw lines all the way around, a circle on the surface of the globe with you as the center. That's the horizon. That's all the world you can see. But. The line of your sight continues past that point where it meets the earth-circle, see? And goes out into space. If you draw another, bigger circle representing just the edge of the atmosphere, see, it's bigger. And all this, above, and back here, this great big bowl, we can see from where we stand. But the earth—or the ocean—only this much. See? So the sky is apparently bigger than any earth we can see. Even the ocean.

STIPAN: The ocean is bigger.

YOUNG ALMA: But look, the diagram—

STIPAN: In the diagram, the sky is bigger. In the middle of the ocean, the ocean is bigger.

YOUNG ALMA: How?

STIPAN: Because you cannot by mistake fall into the sky. Something you might fall into and die is bigger than a thing you only stand and look at. Who taught you this in school?

YOUNG ALMA: Nobody. It just makes sense when you think about it.

(Beat)

STIPAN: Go inside now.

YOUNG ALMA: Papa, what?

STIPAN: Draws a picture to show me the world is round.

YOUNG ALMA: Papa—

STIPAN: Never in my life would I dare to speak to my Papa like that. I'd have sooner crossed the ocean by myself. I did. Than dare that.

YOUNG ALMA: Oh. Oh, I'm sorry, Papa. I am so sorry.

(Beat)

STIPAN: How old are children when they go away to college?

YOUNG ALMA: I'm happy here, Papa.

STIPAN: No you're not. You couldn't be.

YOUNG ALMA: I should go help Mama get ready for bed, excuse me.

STIPAN: Alma.

(She rubs out her drawing.)

YOUNG ALMA: I'm sorry I spoke to you the way I did, I'll never do it again, I promise.

(The lights crossfade to:)

(Japan, 1980s)

(ALMA enters, holding an unlit cigarette and her cell phone. Elsewhere sits EUGENE, in Eastern clothes suitable for sitting zazen, facing outward, away from ALMA, in half-lotus position, very still.)

ALMA: *(On the phone)* Moshi moshi. Yes, I'll hold. *(She takes out her Zippo, strikes it, and lights up.)*

(JOEY *enters, wearing a blue business suit and a power tie. And his Walkman, to which he is bopping fast while playing his Gameboy.*)

(JOEY *and* ALMA *see each other.*)

ALMA *and* JOEY: *(Pointing)* Busted.

ALMA: Hey, *I'm* on the phone. I can't believe you volunteered to come along today.

JOEY: Why not? I love it here, it's awesome.

ALMA: *This* is awesome? I can never predict.

JOEY: *(Restlessly)* I thought the Golden Gate Bridge was old. But this, Jeez. The odometer's turned over a few times on this joint. And it's so still.

ALMA: How would you know, look at you. *(On the phone)* Hideo-san, *hai, konnichi wa.*

(As ALMA *talks,* JOEY *looks outward. He steals a glance at* EUGENE. *He puts away the Gameboy and takes out a guidebook. He opens it and reads.)*

ALMA: *(On the phone)* Here is a thought which has been discussed. What if the parts were assembled in your remarkably efficient plant here after having been made by our workers in, say, Tennessee. *Hai. Hai.* This is just an idea which has emerged from conversations among our people. *Eh. Eh.* See what emerges from your conversation. Good. Good. *Arigato gozaimashita. Sayonara. (She hangs up.)* It was my idea okay, mine, I had it, mememe and I told it to you, now howsaboutit? Like it? Good, done. This is why your mother has been trapped over here for years. It's like after World War Two they said, oh, you didn't like Japanese aggression, okay, see how you like this, Japanese passive aggression, oh my God would you just bomb Hawaii so I'll know what you think?

JOEY: I like them.

ALMA: You want 'em, you got 'em. I like them too, when I don't have to negotiate with them. Unfortunately negotiating is what I am in this world to do.

JOEY: Man.

ALMA: What are you listening to?

JOEY: "Remember, O monks, that all of this world is on fire."

ALMA: Australian rock 'n' roll?

JOEY: *(Holding out the book)* The Buddha.

ALMA: Oh, him.

JOEY: *(Reading)* "And what, O monks, are all these things that are on fire? The eye is on fire; forms are on fire; things seen by the eye are on fire; and whatever feeling depends on things seen by the eye, that too is on fire. And with what are these on fire? With the fire of passion, say I; with the fire of hatred, the fire of obsession; with birth, old age, death, misery, grief and despair, they are on fire." Man. Buddha rocks.

ALMA: *(Pointing outward)* Yeah, there's a bunch of them now.

JOEY: "The ear is on fire: Sounds are on fire. The nose is on fire—"

ALMA: I think I got it.

JOEY: *(Pointing)* And *that* guy.

(They watch him.)

JOEY: Imagine doing that.

ALMA: *You'd* need a Ritalin as big as the Ritz.

JOEY: I'm not that bad.

ALMA: Smidgen, you're the most restless person I know, and I'm descended from pirates. You can't sit still for one minute.

JOEY: Hey. Can so.

ALMA: Want to bet?

JOEY: You're on. Here.

(He hands her the Walkman. He tries to sit. She listens, tentatively, to the Walkman.)

ALMA: How can you listen to this stupid noise?

JOEY: Shh.

(ALMA aims the headphones at JOEY. He starts moving to the beat. He notices what he's doing.)

ALMA: Gotcha.

JOEY: Mother.

ALMA: Try again.

JOEY: I'm doing it.

ALMA: What.

JOEY: Staying still. I'm doing it now.

ALMA: Honey. Fingers, too.

JOEY: Yeah, okay.

ALMA: Honey? Toes.

JOEY: Right.

ALMA: Smidgen?

JOEY: What.

ALMA: You're flaring your nostrils. In a kind of rhythmic way.

JOEY: Okay.

ALMA: Okay. Starting now. Good. Good. Good—

JOEY: *(Everything moving at once)* Yarraghagickah!

ALMA: Hey. Good try.

(EUGENE starts laughing.)

EUGENE: Sorry. I'm sorry. You people are hilarious. *(He totally loses it.)*

(ALMA and JOEY look at each other. She takes out her cell phone. He takes out his Gameboy.)

ALMA: That is not how I pictured a Zen master acting.

EUGENE: Do I look like a Zen master? I'm on a travel grant from S M U. Masters in Comparative Religion.

ALMA: Congratulations.

EUGENE: Thanks, yeah, it's a great opportunity. Though that's not a very Zen way to think.

ALMA: May I ask, in an economy like this, what you do with a Masters in Comparative Religion?

EUGENE: Pray. *(He laughs again.)*

ALMA: Nice to meet you.

EUGENE: Nice to meet y'all. *(He resumes his meditative position.)*

(ALMA sees JOEY playing.)

ALMA: Hey, Smidgen? How's the job?

(JOEY shrugs. He turns back to his game. ALMA goes to look over his shoulder. He notices.)

JOEY: *(Re the game)* It's these two little guys, Italian guys, like masons or something, Luigi and something. The Mario Brothers. Want to try it?

ALMA: No, thank you, dear. Little workers running around with monsters chasing after them, it's like all my nightmares, waiting for Papa to get home safe.

(Lights up on:)

(Wyoming, 1940s)

(STIPAN sits on a kitchen chair in the gravel. He holds a cheap pistol, looking down at it.)

JOEY: Okay, hang on.

ALMA: United Mine Workers.

JOEY: Right.

(ALMA watches JOEY as he plays.)

(YOUNG ALMA runs in, carrying school books. She sees STIPAN and stops, frightened.)

STIPAN: You are early.

YOUNG ALMA: I'm late. I'm sorry. Had to get the school paper to the printer's.

STIPAN: Mm.

(Beat)

YOUNG ALMA: Should I do Mama's exercises before I make supper?

STIPAN: Yes. Go inside now.

(She does not move.)

STIPAN: One of our men smuggled it onto the picket line, opening his coat to show it to his friends, making noise about if they bring in the scabs, oh boy, he's ready.

YOUNG ALMA: Why do you have it, Papa?

STIPAN: He gave it to me. *(Taking the gun to pieces, slamming each piece to the ground at his feet.)* Goddamn cowboys and Indians.

YOUNG ALMA: He gave you his gun?

STIPAN: Mm.

YOUNG ALMA: Why?

STIPAN: I told him to.

YOUNG ALMA: Did *you* have a gun?

(STIPAN *snorts.*)

YOUNG ALMA: But... How did you get him to give you his gun?

(STIPAN *picks up the pieces of pistol.*)

STIPAN: He knew who I was. *(He stands.)*

YOUNG ALMA: Papa? Where are you going?

STIPAN: For a walk. To bury these things.

(JOSEPHINA *limps in on her crutches.*)

STIPAN: Do your Mama's exercises.

JOSEPHINA: Stipan?

(STIPAN *goes.*)

JOSEPHINA: Where is he going?

YOUNG ALMA: For a walk.

JOSEPHINA: Hm.

YOUNG ALMA: *(Indicating the chair)* It's time, Mama.

JOSEPHINA: Ach.*(She sits in the chair.)* Walking for no reason? (JOSEPHINA *looks at* YOUNG ALMA. *Beat)* The strike must be bad.

(YOUNG ALMA *and* JOSEPHINA *go through* JOSEPHINA's *routine of physical therapy exercises.*)

YOUNG ALMA: Mama?

JOSEPHINA: I am working.

YOUNG ALMA: Mama? What are we?

JOSEPHINA: What?

YOUNG ALMA: What kind of people are we?

JOSEPHINA: Is this a trick question? Like the Immigration?

YOUNG ALMA: No, Mama, no, I just...where are you from?

JOSEPHINA: Why.

YOUNG ALMA: At school now they ask a lot.

JOSEPHINA: Just you?

YOUNG ALMA: No, everybody. Because of the war I think. The boys fight.

JOSEPHINA: We're Americans.

YOUNG ALMA: That's what the boys all say. But then they fight anyway. Where are you from?

JOSEPHINA: A village so small you can not find it on an atlas I do not care how big.

YOUNG ALMA: What country? Italy, right?

JOSEPHINA: Depends on when you are asking.

YOUNG ALMA: Now.

JOSEPHINA: Now...Italy.

YOUNG ALMA: I thought so.

JOSEPHINA: But not the bad parts.

YOUNG ALMA: What about Papa?

JOSEPHINA: I am working.

YOUNG ALMA: *(Working on a flex)* A little further, Mama.

JOSEPHINA: *(Shaking her head)* Mm mm.

YOUNG ALMA: You're doing it.

JOSEPHINA: I can do it if you do not rush.

YOUNG ALMA: I'm not rushing. Now.

JOSEPHINA: Why are you rushing?

YOUNG ALMA: Am I?

JOSEPHINA: Do you have someplace to go?

YOUNG ALMA: No. Jim's coming over to do homework.

JOSEPHINA: We will stop.

YOUNG ALMA: No. We have time.

(They resume.)

YOUNG ALMA: Where is Papa from?

JOSEPHINA: Alma.

(They keep working as:)

(Croatia, 1910)

(Lights up on FATHER LUKA, *kneeling where we left him as* EUGENE. YOUNG STIPAN *enters hurriedly, dressed as an altarboy, carrying vestments.)*

FATHER LUKA: You have been seeing the *Amerikanac.*

YOUNG STIPAN: Yes, Father.

*(*YOUNG STIPAN *helps* FATHER LUKA *dress for Mass.)*

FATHER LUKA: He has been telling you about America?

YOUNG STIPAN: And about here, too.

FATHER LUKA: Good. Good. This is a famous place, you know.

YOUNG STIPAN: Yes, Father.

FATHER LUKA: Shakespeare wrote a play about this place.

YOUNG STIPAN: Shakespeare?

FATHER LUKA: I've told you about Shakespeare.

YOUNG STIPAN: Yes, Father.

FATHER LUKA: He also wrote a couple about the Venetians.

YOUNG STIPAN: God damn Venetians.

FATHER LUKA: And what happens to an African who passes through there. And another about a Jew who passes through there.

YOUNG STIPAN: God damn Jews.

FATHER LUKA: One of his plays happens right here.

YOUNG STIPAN: Here in Dalmatia?

FATHER LUKA: They called it Illyria then.

JOSEPHINA: *(To* YOUNG ALMA*)* Your father's little village is right now in Yugoslavia.

YOUNG ALMA: What part of Yugoslavia?

JOSEPHINA: The beautiful part. He tells me.

(FATHER LUKA *and* YOUNG STIPAN *exit.)*

YOUNG ALMA: What part is that?

JOSEPHINA: Are you that radio man, now, that tracer of lost persons?

YOUNG ALMA: A lot of things are happening in Yugoslavia. In school we have maps, the teachers put pins—

JOSEPHINA: I see the maps, in the paper, your Papa shows me the maps.

YOUNG ALMA: What part is he from? What is he?

(JOSEPHINA *grabs her crutches.)*

YOUNG ALMA: Mama, what are you doing—

JOSEPHINA: He is your Papa. Is what he is. Who got out of the old country in 1910, when it was not even the same old country as this new country where all the trouble is. It is not the same place. And besides he left. He is not there. He is not one of them and never was, that is why he left.

YOUNG ALMA: One of who?

(JOSEPHINA *slaps* YOUNG ALMA *across the face.*)

JOSEPHINA: Do you understand me. Do you.

(YOUNG ALMA *nods.* JOSEPHINA *exits.*)

(ALMA *is sitting watching* JOEY *play, phone to her ear.* EUGENE *is back, sitting. A low battery signal beeps.* ALMA *and* JOEY *both check their devices.* ALMA *shuts her phone.*)

ALMA: That's it for me.

JOEY: You look tired, Mom.

ALMA: No business being tired, all I do all day is talk on the phone. Hey, Smidgen?

(ALMA *kneels and draws a circle in the gravel with her finger. She illustrates as she speaks.* JOEY *tries not to fidget.*)

ALMA: Grandpa and Grandma started here, on the Mediterranean. Italy, Croatia. Came west, here, to Wyoming. I went west, here, to California. And had you. You and I came here, westward to the Far East, to Japan. The land of opportunity is a country that moves around. It's gone half way around the world, in just this century. With our people—yours and mine—chasing after it. Do something, Joey? For God's sake. Do something.

(ALMA *exits.* JOEY *starts putting his toys away in various pockets and getting back in business mode.*)

EUGENE: Hey.

(JOEY *looks over.*)

EUGENE: "The body is on fire. Things tangible are on fire. The mind is on fire. Ideas are on fire."

JOEY: Yeah.

(*The lights fade.*)

(Croatia, 1910)

*(*MISS ADAMIC *enters, carrying her boat. She kneels and sets it floating.)*

*(*YOUNG STIPAN *enters, carrying baskets, and stops, looking around.* MISS ADAMIC *glances at* YOUNG STIPAN, *who does not notice her.* MARIJA *enters, carrying baskets, and does.)*

MARIJA: She's over there.

YOUNG STIPAN: Who?

MARIJA: Oh, now she's a "who"? If you've started ignoring each other, this has gone farther than I thought. The ship owner's girl, that's who, the skinny thing with the sailor suit and the boat, what is she supposed to be, advertising? Every market day, the mother goes into all the shops and the girl plays with that damned boat. While decent children are working.

YOUNG STIPAN: *(Still looking around)* There's a man who walks here sometimes. I wanted you to meet him.

MARIJA: Everybody here I know since before you were born.

YOUNG STIPAN: He's from America. He's from here, but he's come back from America.

MARIJA: From this town?

YOUNG STIPAN: A different town, up the coast, I forget.

MARIJA: Why isn't he in his town? He comes all the way back from America to the wrong town?

YOUNG STIPAN: Maybe his town is gone. He's really old. Or it's different now. Or he likes this one better. He knows the Bay of Viganj, he knows every rock.

MARIJA: How did you find that out?

STIPAN: I took him along.

MARIJA: Without asking?

STIPAN: He's old. I thought I should be respectful. Did I do wrong?

MARIJA: Now you want me to meet him.

YOUNG STIPAN: I don't know, he's interesting.

MARIJA: I've got enough interesting in my life. So do you. You've got the priest to talk to.

YOUNG STIPAN: So does he, he talks to the priest, they tell stories.

MARIJA: He's made friends with the priest.

YOUNG STIPAN: Here he comes.

(IVO *enters.*)

YOUNG STIPAN: Mister Pasic!

IVO: Good day, Stipan.

(*They shake hands.*)

YOUNG STIPAN: This is my mother.

IVO: An honor.

MARIJA: Oh ha.

IVO: Ivo Pasic. I congratulate you on your splendid son.

MARIJA: I know he's splendid, I'm around him all the time. He's in love with you, too. Tell me about the streets. The American streets.

IVO: The streets?

MARIJA: Gold, yes? Paved with gold.

IVO: I have told you no such thing, have I?

MARIJA: Thank God at least for that.

IVO: Of course not. If they paved the streets with gold, gold wouldn't be worth anything. But I know how that rumor got started. In a place where a person wakes up in his own home and goes to work that is well paid and

worthwhile, the very pavement where he walks will
seem to shine.

MARIJA: Oh ho ho. When I was a girl, tinkers would
come to town and use a tongue like that to talk stupid
girls into a thin-bottomed pot and a night in the fields.

IVO: But never you, I bet.

MARIJA: No.

IVO: I shed a tear for the tinkers of the world.

MARIJA: So if it's such a paradise, America, why aren't
you there?

IVO: America was a paradise to me, yes. I did many
things there. But I find I'm done with doing. I'm an old
man. I just want to be. But America never lets you be.

MARIJA: How long will you be staying here?

IVO: Not long. I think I would enjoy another passage.
I used to resent the time between places. But lately,
I find, shipboard time suits me. The steamships swing
back and forth across the Atlantic like a pendulum
in the casket of a clock. In the clock of the ocean, the
waves are seconds, the tides are days, the ships cross
every fortnight. Back and forth. Outside the clock,
time goes forward, around and around. I say, let it.

MARIJA: What the hell is happening here? *(To* YOUNG
STIPAN*)* What are you doing?

IVO: Madam, if—

MARIJA: *(To* IVO*)* Not you. Him. *(To* YOUNG STIPAN*)*
Tell me what you're doing. Say it to me. Say it!

IVO: Madam—

MARIJA: *(To* IVO*)* Him! *(To* YOUNG STIPAN*)* What do you
want to do!

YOUNG STIPAN: *(Mumbled)* America.

MARIJA: What about it!

YOUNG STIPAN: To go there.

(She shoves him off his feet.)

MARIJA: Who! Who! Who!

YOUNG STIPAN: Me?

MARIJA: *(To* YOUNG STIPAN*)* And who are you, thinking you know what my son wants! Like you've been watching you, closer than I have! Stand up! Stand! What's the matter with you! You think you can get across the ocean and live in a country full of strangers when you can't say a word to your mother who loves you!

YOUNG STIPAN: What do you want me to say?

MARIJA: What you want!

YOUNG STIPAN: I want to go to America.

MARIJA: Son, I have a question for your new friend.

IVO: Anything, madam. Living conditions in America? The morals of the young people? The safety of available jobs? What can I tell you to help ease your natural concerns?

MARIJA: What's your commission?

IVO: I'm sorry, madam, I...?

MARIJA: How much do you get per man you bring over?

YOUNG STIPAN: Mother, what are you—

MARIJA: How much is he worth to you? If I offer you the same, would you piss off out of my town?

YOUNG STIPAN: Mother, he's retired, you heard him.

MARIJA: I heard him.

IVO: He'll go anyway.

MARIJA: Satisfy a mother's curiosity.

IVO: The steamship company does subsidize my
passage, and a quite reputable employment agency
does defray some of the expenses of my journey, in
exchange for which, if I should meet a young man or
two whose minds are already made up for America,
I show them the ropes. Everyone benefits.

MARIJA: Almost everyone.

IVO: You as well. The money he can earn in America
will—

MARIJA: This isn't my Christmas pig, old man. I didn't
raise him for you or any other butcher.

YOUNG STIPAN: Mother?

IVO: Come now, madam. How many families in this
village would be off their land by now if it weren't for
money from boys like this in America? How many
years has this town been propped up by nothing but
dollars? Your sons are your only cash crop that anyone
is willing to buy!

YOUNG STIPAN: Sir?

IVO: Isn't that so?

MARIJA: Son. You've just had your first lesson in
American. What have you learned? Well?

YOUNG STIPAN: I'm sorry.

MARIJA: I'm sorry? *(She strikes him.)* You could have
died! *(She strikes him.)* I thought you had sense! I'm
sorry? *(She strikes him.)* How am I supposed to keep
you alive with the sense God gave a sheep!

(The bell rings.)

MARIJA: Go! Run ahead! Tell him I was haggling long!

YOUNG STIPAN: He'll ask why I didn't stay to help carry things.

(She hands him a basket.)

MARIJA: Here!

(He runs out. She quickly gathers the rest of her things.)

IVO: Perhaps I should speak to Stipan's father.

MARIJA: Not if you want the boy alive. Listen to me, my husband would like the idea of his going, but he'd beat the boy to death for having thought of it himself. Stay away, you hear me?

IVO: Now I understand why you want to keep him for yourself.

MARIJA: You don't understand a thing.

IVO: He's getting bigger and stronger. One day soon the father goes to beat him, or somebody else, and the boy will beat the father instead. And the beatings will stop.

MARIJA: You know nothing.

IVO: Only what I've seen. I am from here. You think I don't know the look of a Croat woman waiting for someone to grow strong? What will he have to do before you let him go?

(MARIJA runs out as the lights fade.)

(Wyoming, 1940s)

(Distant through static we hear East St. Louis Toodle-Oo. YOUNG ALMA *and* JIM, *a high school boy, jitterbug.)*

JOSEPHINA: *(Calling, off)* Alma?

YOUNG ALMA: *(To* JIM*)* Sorry. *(Calling)* We're studying, Mama!

JOSEPHINA: *(Calling, off)* I'm sure Jim didn't come over here—

(YOUNG ALMA *joins her under her breath.*)

JOSEPHINA: *(Calling, off)* —just so you could listen to stupid noise! Hello, Jim!

JIM: *(Calling)* I'm fine, ma'am, thanks!

JOSEPHINA: *(Calling, off)* What did you say, Jim?

(Y OUNG ALMA *growls softly and turns off the radio.*)

YOUNG ALMA: *(Calling)* Mama, do you need anything?

JOSEPHINA: *(Calling, off)* Now I am okay!

YOUNG ALMA: Sorry.

JIM: It's okay. I like *your* parents.

YOUNG ALMA: You want 'em you got 'em.

JIM: At least they speak English.

YOUNG ALMA: I still can't understand them.

JIM: I can always tell what they're saying.

YOUNG ALMA: What they're *saying*. What they *mean* is a mystery.

JIM: Like what.

YOUNG ALMA: Like anything. Where they're from? Europe, I'm pretty sure it's Europe. Where are you from, Jim?

JIM: Rock Springs, same as you.

YOUNG ALMA: Right. How hard was *that*? To hear them talk, Europe's this *Alice In Wonderland* continent, the people stay put and the countries move around. At least you know what you are.

JIM: Listen, my folks, the minute something goes wrong they start yelling about going back to the old country.

YOUNG ALMA: Like how?

JIM: Like my report card wasn't so great today.

YOUNG ALMA: Pfister, right? Pfister's a Nazi.

JIM: What'd he give you?

YOUNG ALMA: Oh, who cares, he's a big Nazi.

JIM: You aced it, didn't you.

YOUNG ALMA: No I did not.

JIM: Meaning what, an A-minus? *(Beat)* You're kidding.

YOUNG ALMA: I can't help it! They give me these *grades*.
So Pfister creamed you and what did your parents do?

JIM: They actually got down suitcases and started
packing. I'm yelling in Italian, trying to explain, did
I mention I have to speak this foreign language in my
own home? My sisters are crying, begging not to go
back—back! Mom and Pop saying, "We'll go back!"
like this is a place us kids have ever *been*! The sisters,
it's a horror movie, all those stories of my Mom's, the
sisters figure in the old country they'd never leave the
house and I'll have to knife any guy goes near them.
So they're begging to stay here, and that makes it
worse, 'cause now Pop figures they want to grow up
to be bad American women. And the worst thing—
these people, waving their arms, yelling at each other
in this useless Sicilian dialect—and the worst
thing—everything they say about us is true.

YOUNG ALMA: Are they really taking you back?

JIM: To *Sicilia*? Sicily! Damn Italian coming out of my
mouth. Patton and Montgomery are in Sicily, I don't
think the folks will be going. I don't care what they do.

YOUNG ALMA: What'll you do?

JIM: I'm quitting school.

YOUNG ALMA: You can't.

JIM: Watch me.

YOUNG ALMA: One bad report card, Jim—

JIM: I'm quitting school and joining up.

(Beat)

YOUNG ALMA: Jim.

JIM: I'm joining the Army Air Corps. Next week I'm on the train to Lubbock, Texas, and learning to fly. They won't let Italians go to Europe as ground troops, but they'll let you volunteer to fly. And I'm going over there and I'm going to drop a whole bunch of bombs on Sicily. I'll show them.

YOUNG ALMA: Who? What's that going to prove? Jimmy, that could be your family down there.

JIM: Yeah, well. They had their chance.

(Beat. JIM *takes out a pack of cigarettes and a stainless-steel Zippo lighter.)*

YOUNG ALMA: *Gee.*

*(*JIM *strikes the lighter on the seam of his jeans and lights up.)*

YOUNG ALMA: *Gee.*

JIM: You want one?

YOUNG ALMA: Oh, I would never smoke. Can I see the lighter?

JIM: Oh, right. Science Girl.

(He hands it to her.)

YOUNG ALMA: It's neat.

JIM: Thanks.

(She tries to light it the way he did.)

JIM: *(Genially)* You dope. Here. *(He shows her. He gives it back to her. She holds it.)*

YOUNG ALMA: You're going? Really going?

JIM: You're leaving too.

YOUNG ALMA: No I'm not.

JIM: Aren't you? Everybody figures you're going away to college.

YOUNG ALMA: Stop. Everybody, please, just—

JIM: What?

YOUNG ALMA: Who do we know who's gone away to college? Nobody goes away to college.

JIM: Yeah. But everybody thinks *you* will.

YOUNG ALMA: They think I could just leave my mother sitting there. They think I could leave here and never come back.

JIM: Don't tell me you'd miss this town.

YOUNG ALMA: Not the town.

JIM: What does your mother think?

YOUNG ALMA: God knows what my mother thinks. And God is not telling. Believe me, I ask Him a lot. I'm not going anywhere. Who will I have to talk to?

JIM: You talk to lots of people.

YOUNG ALMA: And talk and talk, God, I wish I could do something to just shut up.

(He kisses her.)

YOUNG ALMA: Oh.

(He kisses her again. They come up for air. He is smiling.)

YOUNG ALMA: What.

JIM: What?

YOUNG ALMA: The look on your face.

JIM: What?

YOUNG ALMA: Like you just won a bet or something.

JIM: Like I won something?

YOUNG ALMA: Yeah. Why?

JIM: You dope. *(He kisses her again.)*

YOUNG ALMA: Do you really have to go?

JIM: Yeah.

YOUNG ALMA: You're sure? MI(She kisses him.)

JIM: Yeah.

YOUNG ALMA: You're really sure? *(She kisses him.)*

JIM: Alma, come on, don't—

YOUNG ALMA: What—

JIM: I can't—I've got to—

YOUNG ALMA: Got to what? *(She kisses him.)*

JIM: To *go*, and—

(She kisses him.)

JIM: I know you want me to stay and I want to stay but I want to go and what'll I—I can't want 'em both at once, I don't—

YOUNG ALMA: *(Between little kisses)* Okay. Okay. Don't. I know.

JIM: You got me confused, there.

YOUNG ALMA: I'm sorry. *(Pleasantly surprised)* I did?

JIM: Yeah.

(They are holding hands.)

YOUNG ALMA: Look. One of us has to stay here. Maybe it can be me.

JIM: Why?

YOUNG ALMA: You dope. One of us has to wait for the other one.

JIM: Oh.

(They kiss, long.)

YOUNG ALMA: I wonder if it is true, what they say about us.

JIM: Us who.

YOUNG ALMA: *Paisans.*

JIM: What do they say about us?

YOUNG ALMA: That we're like this.

(She kisses him. He pulls back.)

YOUNG ALMA: What. What, Jim? What'd I do?

JIM: We're not what they say. *I'm* not.

YOUNG ALMA: Oh, I don't even know what I'm talking about.

JIM: I'll show them I'm not.

(She takes his hand. They stand like that.)

MARIJA: *(Off, fast)* O my God I am heartily sorry for having offended thee.

(The lights fade:)

(Croatia, 1910)

(In darkness:)

MARIJA: *(Fast)* And I detest all my sins because of thy just punishments.

(Dim light on two faces.)

MARIJA: I firmly resolve with the help of thy grace to sin no more and to avoid the near occasion of sin Amen. It has been one week since my last confession.

*(The sound of a wooden frame sliding. Light through mesh
that separates two faces,* MARIJA's *and* FATHER LUKA's.*)*

FATHER LUKA: What sins do you wish to confess?

MARIJA: I have committed the sin of anger by wishing
someone dead.

FATHER LUKA: Who?

MARIJA: You, you idiot. This is all your fault.

FATHER LUKA: Mine?

MARIJA: You started it. Books. Jason and the Argonauts.

FATHER LUKA: I have taught him something about the
history of his home. Why would that make him wish to
leave it?

MARIJA: The History of Dalmatia: people come here and
rob us or we leave here and go rob somebody else. And
he's here already.

FATHER LUKA: We've never been allowed to defend
ourselves. No one has let us be who we are. I'm trying
to teach the boy about that.

MARIJA: I knew it was your fault.

FATHER LUKA: If you didn't want him to learn, why did
you let him come to me?

MARIJA: I needed something to keep him here. We all
thought you would leave here years ago, and you never
did.

FATHER LUKA: I became a priest.

MARIJA: You read. And you stayed. I thought for him,
too, maybe, the books could take the place of America.
So. You will tell him not to go.

FATHER LUKA: Would that help?

MARIJA: He listens to you.

FATHER LUKA: He listens to me because I never ask him to do something he doesn't want.

MARIJA: Why don't you want to help me?

FATHER LUKA: I want what's best for the boy.

MARIJA: It is best that he stay. Best for everyone. Best for him, best for me, best for you.

FATHER LUKA: Best for me how?

MARIJA: How can I make it best for you?

FATHER LUKA: You seem terribly troubled.

MARIJA: I am about to lose my son forever. How can I get you to help me?

FATHER LUKA: No need, no need. If you wish me to speak with him—

MARIJA: Yes, yes—

FATHER LUKA: —learn the state of his mind—

MARIJA: No! You have to tell him, you can't give up, how can I repay you so you won't give up until he stays.

FATHER LUKA: Nothing, there is nothing.

MARIJA: There must be something, I know this, you deny yourself so long, any pleasure, any happiness. Wanting, it's a habit like anything. What do you want?

FATHER LUKA: I don't—

MARIJA: Listen. I know. I see what you've done to him.

FATHER LUKA: I told you—

MARIJA: You are not like other men here, now neither is he. Teaching him about the Greeks. I should have stopped it, but now— Listen. Make him stay. I'll give him to you.

FATHER LUKA: Give him to me?

MARIJA: He could be one of you. I wouldn't care.

FATHER LUKA: One of us.

MARIJA: He lives to please you, keep him here and he'll be whatever you want.

FATHER LUKA: What I want.

MARIJA: He's good, loving, a loving sweet boy, so shy, gentle, he burns up in the sun, the farm girls want to eat him alive.

FATHER LUKA: No boy is quite the way his mother sees him.

MARIJA: He is, he is still such a boy, he still sleeps like a little boy, sweet not sour like a man. He rubs his fists in his eyes when he's waking up, like a little boy. You'll see.

FATHER LUKA: I think you are mistaken about me, madam.

MARIJA: Why. How.

FATHER LUKA: I have tried to help your son.

MARIJA: And he's taken to it, hasn't he?

FATHER LUKA: But I have not been working to make him a priest.

MARIJA: A priest. No.

FATHER LUKA: No. You are mistaken about me. I want nothing but his success in life. And you are mistaken about us, us priests, the boy you describe, that gentle boy, the life of a priest is not for the gentle, we have to be men.

MARIJA: Yes, of course, I didn't mean—

FATHER LUKA: We have to be at least as strong as other men if we hope to change their ways.

MARIJA: Yes, yes, I see. You are more like other men than I thought.

FATHER LUKA: Yes. I think your son is as well.

MARIJA: I was mistaken. I see now.

FATHER LUKA: Good.

MARIJA: I thought there was something in him you wanted. But I see now. You want something else entirely. I know. We could do that. Just say you will. Just say. Say I'll think.

FATHER LUKA: I'll think.

MARIJA: And you'll save my boy. For me. Well?

FATHER LUKA: Of these and any other sins you may have committed I absolve you in the name of the Father and the Son and the Holy Spirit, Amen.

MARIJA: The penance, you forgot the penance.

FATHER LUKA: Say a rosary.

MARIJA: Let me know.

(The lights fade up.)

(Japan, 1980s)

(ALMA and EUGENE are sitting just where MARIJA and FATHER LUKA were. JOEY stands at a distance, no Walkman, no Gameboy, no phone.)

ALMA: *(On the phone)* I'm telling you, it's the only place that still has that good old American get up and go. Japan. Think about it. *(She hangs up.)*

JOEY: How long was that?

ALMA: What? I lost track.

JOEY: A long time.

ALMA: We weren't betting that time.

(He shrugs.)

JOEY: Whatever.

(He strolls away. ALMA watches.)

EUGENE: *(To ALMA)* Are you okay?

ALMA: Sure. Thanks. *(She flips open her phone. Then she stops and looks at it.)* Yes and no.

EUGENE: That's a good Zen answer.

ALMA: I guess I could use a spiritual advisor, but I'm afraid you're the wrong flavor.

EUGENE: What's your flavor?

ALMA: I was raised Catholic.

EUGENE: Hey, me too.

(They share a smile.)

ALMA: Why'd you leave?

EUGENE: Gay. You?

ALMA: Divorced. You know what I wish? More than anything.

EUGENE: That something could make him happy.

ALMA: Ha. That should be it, shouldn't it. No, I was wishing I could be some tough old-world peasant mother so I could make him be happy. No doubt by slapping him silly. Which is worse: finding out you've become your mother, or finding out you can't?

EUGENE: I wonder sometimes what kind of priest I would have made. Do all of us wonder that? A Jesuit, maybe. Curious about other religions. A whiff of taboo under the collar.

ALMA: I'd be a matriarch. And I'd know what to say.

EUGENE: What do you think you'd say?

ALMA: What do good old-world Catholics say?

EUGENE & ALMA: *(Together)* O my God I am heartily sorry—

(They look at each other and crack up. Beat. He nods to her.)

ALMA: O my God I am heartily sorry for having offended thee...

(A deep bell rings.)

EUGENE: Saved by the bell.

(He stands. The bell rings.)

ALMA: *(Rattled)* What the *hell*.

EUGENE: They're calling us to meditation.

(The bell rings.)

ALMA: Oh, worse and worse.

EUGENE: What's wrong?

(The bell rings. STIPAN enters and stands, listening.)

STIPAN: Alma!

ALMA: That's the cave-in signal.

EUGENE: The what?

(The bell rings. YOUNG ALMA runs in and stands with her father.)

YOUNG ALMA: I hear, Papa.

(The bell rings.)

ALMA: The church bells rang like that when the men in the mines had pushed their luck and the earth had given way. So the women would either be grieving or cooking for the neighbors.

(The bell rings.)

JOSEPHINA: *(Calling, off)* Stipan!

(YOUNG STIPAN *enters, at a run, trying to carry too many baskets.*)

(*The bell rings.* JOSEPHINA *limps in.*)

EUGENE: Ma'am, I should get ready...

ALMA: A cave-in was like Halloween in reverse: ghosts inside the house and kids bringing food to the doorstep.

(*The bell rings.* YOUNG ALMA *runs out.*)

ALMA: Always hated that sound.

(YOUNG STIPAN *runs out. The bell rings.*)

STIPAN: Always hated that sound.

(STIPAN, ALMA, JOSEPHINA, *and* EUGENE *cross themselves and exit.*)

(*Leaving, alone on stage, standing at a slightly awkward angle as if caught by a sudden thought and held there,* JOEY. *Absolutely still. Silence.*)

(JOEY *stays absolutely still for a really noticeable period of time. Then he blinks and looks around. He smiles.*)

JOEY: *Yeah.*

(*Blackout*)

END OF ACT ONE

ACT TWO

(Japan, 1980s)

(ALMA, *in a business suit, stands on one foot with a matching pump in her hand.*)

ALMA: How do these gravels always get in my shoes?

JOEY: *(Calling softly, off)* Hush, Mom, okay? A little softer?

ALMA: Sorry, right. Two steps and I might as well be barefoot out here. They jump up. Look at that, you take a step, they jump up right into the shoe. I'm treading lightly, watch, and—yep, yep—no matter what you do they jump up and bite you. These stockings are for the rag drawer already. God, and look at these heels. Every time I come, I sacrifice a pair of Ferragamos to Buddha.

(JOEY *enters, dressed as a Zen Buddhist novice. Beat*)

JOEY: Do you mind a lot?

ALMA: What's a lot?

JOEY: I thought so.

ALMA: Listen, Smidgen, you're doing me a favor. I tell people, oh, yes, my son is here, I am encouraging him to study here, he is fascinated by your disciplines and culture. Well. They all send a kid to America, and none of us returns the favor, it pisses them off, they think we're not really committed to their market, they literally expect you to sacrifice your first-born. So no, I don't mind, you're scoring me big points here.

JOEY: I knew you minded.

ALMA: Oh, don't be your Dad, do not be your Dad,
I'll cry all over the Great Kyoto Desert here. Place still
reminds me of the Sheraton Atlanta, why is that?
Remember the Petersons? Back in—where—

JOEY: Seattle? San Jose?

ALMA: Sacramento. Across the street four houses down?

JOEY: Billy Peterson. I played with him.

ALMA: With the front yard like this.

JOEY: I remember.

ALMA: Gravel, three aloe plants, two lava rocks, call it
a day? A long time the rest of us thought, you know,
when's he gonna *start*? Panel truck full of sod, let's go!
It finally dawned on us—he *is* done. That's the street,
remember? Lawn, lawn, lawn, strip mine, lawn. Wes
Hodges—remember the Hodgeses? Older couple—

JOEY: Across the street from the Petersons?

ALMA: Wanted to kill the Petersons. Said they'd always
thought they'd retire to Arizona, they went down to
take a look, caught the next flight back, said the whole
place looked like Peterson's yard.

JOEY: How are they doing?

ALMA: Lost touch with them. Lost touch with most of
them. Listen, bucko, I know you're trying to live in the
eternal present here, but we've got to make some plans.

JOEY: Plans about what?

ALMA: Plans about leaving. The office is up and
running, we've imported and headhunted and hired
a credible permanent staff.

JOEY: But you're the head of the staff.

ALMA: Smidgen, I'm the fireman. That's what I do.

JOEY: Where? Back to the States?

ALMA: Maybe. I don't know yet.

JOEY: I was hoping maybe this time you'd be staying on.

(Beat)

ALMA: May I smoke in your presence, your Holiness?

JOEY: You shouldn't smoke.

ALMA: I know that I shouldn't, I'm asking if I may.

JOEY: Yes, you may.

(She does.)

ALMA: Oh, *that's* why I keep thinking of the Sheraton
Atlanta, the lobby, years ago, the lobby in the old days,
they had these big ashtrays that looked just like this.
I'm looking up like Buddha's gonna strike me dead.
But he doesn't work like that, does he.

JOEY: No.

ALMA: He waits. It's a lot about waiting, this religion.
The thing about a garden, a real garden, forgive me
I know this is a real garden, so far for me it's the
Emperor's New Garden, I'm afraid I'm gonna go,
Look at the beautiful *plants*! I also keep thinking I
stay here long enough I'll get it. Is that the thing?

JOEY: It is and it isn't.

ALMA: There's also a lot of that in this religion.
(She flicks her ash into the palm of her free hand.)

JOEY: *(Re the ash)* It's okay.

ALMA: Hey, I'm not an animal. I could never go for
such a wishy-washy belief system. With Catholicism,
you've got the Pope, and the thing about Popes is they
are always basically the same, they're always basically
wrong, so you always know where you stand.

JOEY: Where you stand.

ALMA: You stand shrugging in bemusement, that's where you stand, they call him *Il Papa* 'cause he's dumb as your parents. I mean, everybody's parents, I mean me too. They'll never accept you here.

JOEY: They've accepted you.

ALMA: No. I'm a woman. I have a leg up because they think I'm Jewish, and I don't always correct them.

JOEY: Why is that an advantage?

ALMA: They're incredibly racist here, haven't you noticed? They say things educated people never permit themselves to say anymore in the States outside of a country club. They think all Jews are financial wizards, and I can pass. I'm accepted on the same terms as any immigrant anywhere: They can use what I do. Period. And you're trying to do nothing. So.

JOEY: It's not nothing.

ALMA: It's not something, either.

JOEY: That's right. You know how hard that is to do? All at once?

ALMA: This religion, it drives me crazy this religion, it's like op art, you look at it your brain goes wonky!

JOEY: You could stay here too.

ALMA: That's not my job.

JOEY: You could get a different job.

ALMA: Let's see. Me. A superannuated white woman. Cut all ties, lose all seniority. To stay in Japan with you. So you can stick with Zen Buddhism.

JOEY: I guess it's not a practical idea.

ALMA: Thank God. Now—

JOEY: I want to do it anyway.

ALMA: For Zen? For *Zen*?

JOEY: You wanted me to do something!

ALMA: Well, Jesus Christ, I didn't mean *this*! We can't all quit our jobs and go begging in the street with funny hats on. We did not come halfway round the world to give you to the priests! *(Beat)* I can't just leave you sitting here, Joe.

JOEY: I am not just sitting here.

ALMA: Of course you're just sitting there, that's the whole thing with this religion, just sitting there!

JOEY: Could you stop judging me for one second?

ALMA: No.

JOEY: Repeat after me: "Honey, whatever you do is fine with me."

ALMA: You want some other mother.

JOEY: "Because I trust you."

ALMA: You want some Episcopalian mother.

JOEY: "I know you'll do what's best for you."

ALMA: That is not me. *(Beat)* Is that why you're doing this? Make yourself less like me?

JOEY: No. Less like me.

ALMA: Same thing. Sweetie, sweetie, listen. You're okay. You are.

JOEY: No, no—I just don't—

ALMA: Your life is a miracle of sweetness and ease! You are happy! Why don't see you are so happy! Happy! Why do you want to lose your self? It's a great self, I love your self. Why throw it away for nothing? Why go there?

JOEY: Mother. Why *go? Why go?* That's what we *do,* isn't it? Fucking *go? (As he exits:)*

(WYOMING, 1940s)

(STIPAN enters.)

STIPAN: I'm getting you the best education. You are going to Stanford University.

(YOUNG ALMA follows him.)

YOUNG ALMA: It's in California.

STIPAN: It's to the West. It's new out there.

(ALMA exits.)

STIPAN: Same school for boys and girls. Nothing second-class for you. Boys and girls in college learn how to compete. If you learn to compete with college boys, you'll be able to compete with men.

YOUNG ALMA: Papa? Do I have to go away?

(STIPAN looks at her.)

YOUNG ALMA: Why?

(Beat)

STIPAN: Why.

YOUNG ALMA: I know you want me to—

STIPAN: When I was a boy I begged to go. Begged!

YOUNG ALMA: Papa—

STIPAN: We didn't come all this way for you to cut off your options.

(Beat)

YOUNG ALMA: Papa? What if maybe we could think about S M U?

STIPAN: Smu? What is a Smu and why should we think about it.

YOUNG ALMA: It is a very good university. In Texas.

STIPAN: My father beat me for going to the priest to learn to read and you want to move to Texas? Texas is Wyoming without the modesty! What is in Texas for you?

JOSEPHINA: *(Calling, off)* There will be a boy in Texas.

YOUNG ALMA: Oh Mama.

STIPAN: There are boys in California, there's nothing but boys in California, it is the country of boys and girls.

YOUNG ALMA: But Papa, Stanford—

STIPAN: I know, named for a robber baron's boy, can't help that.

YOUNG ALMA: What does Mama think?

JOSEPHINA: *(Calling, off)* Smith College is the best.

STIPAN: Smith College. Back East. The bosses send their children Back East. You know who is sending his boy Back East to an Ivy League college? John L. Lewis. I could not believe it. I said to him, "Do you want your boy to grow up like the bosses?"

YOUNG ALMA: S M U is a nationally known university.

JOSEPHINA: *(Calling, off)* With letters for a name. What do the letters mean?

(Beat)

YOUNG ALMA: Southern Methodist University.

JOSEPHINA: *(A scream, off)* Methodist!?

STIPAN: The subject is over.

JOSEPHINA: *(Off)* Methodist!?

STIPAN: I did not come here so you would have to go to college to be a Protestant.

YOUNG ALMA: You don't have to become a—

JOSEPHINA: *(Off)* Methodist!?

STIPAN: She will not be a Methodist, *cara!*

YOUNG ALMA: Thank you, Papa.

STIPAN: Because she will not do this to herself. This is America. You do not have to be with the priests to learn to read. I ran away to America so my children would be Americans, and be free! Nobody is going to do to you what they did to me.

YOUNG ALMA: What did they do to you, Papa?

STIPAN: You hear me?

(YOUNG ALMA nods. JIM enters.)

JIM: Hi. Good evening, sir.

YOUNG ALMA: Hi. Jim and I are going to work at the library, Papa. I'll get my things. *(Calling)* Do you need anything before I go, Mama?

JOSEPHINA: *(Calling, off)* I need my rosary!

YOUNG ALMA: Isn't it by the bed?

JOSEPHINA: *(Calling, off)* I need it to go around your neck!

YOUNG ALMA: I'll be right back, okay, Papa, don't —

STIPAN: Don't what?

YOUNG ALMA: I don't know, just don't.

(She exits at a run.)

STIPAN: Do you have plans?

JIM: We've got to finish some work for the school paper.

STIPAN: No. I mean— *(A wave toward the distance)*

JIM: Next week I start flight school, sir.

STIPAN: Really. Where?

JIM: Lubbock, Texas, sir.

STIPAN: Texas.

JIM: Yes, sir. Then overseas.

STIPAN: The Pacific?

JIM: I'll fight the Japs if they want me to, sir, but I'm hoping for Europe.

STIPAN: Europe. Hoping to get some Wops? *Paisan*?

(Beat)

JIM: I would, sir.

STIPAN: Italy is finished. Japan is nearly finished too.

JIM: They don't seem to know that.

STIPAN: No. Useful quality.

JIM: Sir, I know this is—but—whose side are you on, anyway? I mean, I'm sure you're as American as the next guy—

STIPAN: In this neighborhood.

JIM: It's none of my business, but I know you, I mean I know your daughter, but if somebody heard you talk like that who didn't know you... They might start thinking. That's all.

STIPAN: About my loyalty. Who I'm loyal to.

JIM: Well.

STIPAN: Because loyal is a good thing to be?

JIM: Well, yes, sir. Somebody disloyal...

STIPAN: What? Stabs his friends in the back?

JIM: Yes, sir.

STIPAN: Loyal people stab strangers all over. Listen, son. Loyalty is not a principle. Loyalty is an excuse to lose every principle.

JIM: But—if you feel that way—how can you be a union man?

STIPAN: The union is not about loyalty. The union is about the principle that a person owns his own labor and has the right to bargain collectively. The day the union becomes about union men's loyalty to each other regardless of principle, that is the day the union will start to die.

(YOUNG ALMA *enters.*)

STIPAN: What about your family, son?

YOUNG ALMA: What's going on?

STIPAN: Do your parents want you to do this?

JIM: *Mia famiglia é Fascista!*

YOUNG ALMA: Papa, stop it, please—

STIPAN: Are you being loyal to them?

JIM: Hell no. Sir.

YOUNG ALMA: Oh God.

(Beat)

STIPAN: All right. Don't stay out too late.

(JIM *does not move.*)

YOUNG ALMA: We're going now.

(JIM *and* YOUNG ALMA *start to go.* YOUNG ALMA *turns back.*)

YOUNG ALMA: I'll be home in time to get Mama down for the night.

STIPAN: Get your schoolwork done.

YOUNG ALMA: I will, but I—

STIPAN: We will be okay.

YOUNG ALMA: Papa? Do you know how to get Mama into bed?

(Beat)

STIPAN: Since before you were born.

YOUNG ALMA: If you're sure. *(She starts to go again.)*

YOUNG ALMA: What, Papa?

STIPAN: Nothing, nothing.

(She runs out.)

JOSEPHINA: *(Off)* You are a very bad man.

(They laugh. STIPAN wipes his eyes. He sits, exhausted. He takes out his pocket watch and looks at it. He turns on the radio.)

RADIO ANNOUNCER: Who knows what evil lurks in the hearts of men?

JOSEPHINA: *(Calling, off)* Alma? Are you still here?

RADIO ANNOUNCER: The Shadow knows....

JOSEPHINA: *(Calling, off)* Your father does not bring you that radio kit all the way—

STIPAN: It's me, *cara*. I like it.

JOSEPHINA: *(Calling, off)* Stipan!?

(STIPAN growls and turns off the radio. JOSEPHINA limps in.)

STIPAN: Do you need anything, *cara*?

JOSEPHINA: *(Looking at the radio)* She does all the work to build this thing for listening to some other place. Why do you bring her this? To teach her that other places is where everything happens?

STIPAN: She said she wanted to give you music.

JOSEPHINA: She did that already. She always did that. *(A laugh)* She tells you it is for *me*? All I hear on it is people shooting people. I do not need a machine for that. That girl. For me, this is? She tells *me* she wants it for *you*, for the news. You talk to her about college.

STIPAN: She says you need her here.

JOSEPHINA: *Me* she tells that I need her here to help me with you. You see what she does? Divide and conquer! That girl, she is *Hitler*.

STIPAN: That sweet girl?

JOSEPHINA: That sweet girl—you are away too much.

STIPAN: How can she know what to want for herself? With both of us to please?

JOSEPHINA: And a boy now.

STIPAN: Yes.

JOSEPHINA: Oh, I am not enough in this country. They like to mix you in. In the old country, the boys like that, they drink, they break things.

STIPAN: What things?

JOSEPHINA: You know. Jewish things. Stipan, what if they send us to some place.

STIPAN: They will not send us anyplace.

JOSEPHINA: They send the Japanese. They say where the Japanese are, it is nothing but shacks and dirt and trees cut down.

STIPAN: They will not send us. He is a boy, *cara*, what he says, it means nothing.

JOSEPHINA: He is a boy, he says what he hears. You think I am afraid for nothing? My Papa brings over me and Marcello, the next year Mama will come with the *bambini*, but they do not let them come.

STIPAN: They didn't need any more of us, *cara*, the labor market—

JOSEPHINA: I am a girl, Stipan, I think it is because the Americans look one time at me and say, "Okay, but that's it."

STIPAN: It was not personal.

JOSEPHINA: "What is wrong with these Italian people they speak English so bad, in America only stupid people speak English so bad, Italian people must be so stupid, we will stop them from coming here—"

STIPAN: Politics, *cara*, talk for people frightened about their job.

JOSEPHINA: My Papa cried on the newspaper. In front of me. 1924. And now the war. How long since we hear they are okay?

STIPAN: They changed the laws. Yes. But we are here.

JOSEPHINA: Oh, you are an American now so you think I am stupid too? They change the laws one time, they can change them again! Yes? So. *What if they send us someplace?*

(Beat)

STIPAN: Then we will go someplace. We have done it before.

JOSEPHINA: Easy for you, you are always going.

STIPAN: It is my work, *cara*.

JOSEPHINA: I am sitting here, I do not care what they say. I am a good Catholic woman, that is what I am to do. Sit here and make a place for my family.

STIPAN: Then I will stay too.

(YOUNG STIPAN comes in, carrying his book, and sits, staring into the distance.)

JOSEPHINA: No. You will go to them and fight about it. To make them change it. I know you.

(The lights fade.)

(Croatia, 1910)

*(*MISS ADAMIC *enters with her boat. She puts it in the water.)*

MISS ADAMIC: You don't look at me the way you used to.

YOUNG STIPAN: Ah. Um, good afternoon.

MISS ADAMIC: Good afternoon. Why don't you?

YOUNG STIPAN: I didn't mean to stare.

MISS ADAMIC: It upset my mother very much. She asked me all sorts of questions about you.

YOUNG STIPAN: I didn't mean to make trouble for you. I won't do it again.

MISS ADAMIC: I wish you would.

YOUNG STIPAN: You—why?

MISS ADAMIC: Mira Radalj got stared at by a farm boy for so long her mother was convinced they were in love. She took Mira to Vienna for almost a year to forget him. Now Mira's engaged to the son of a Hapsburg count. I want to go to Vienna. A girl has so many more opportunities there. My mother went into the pastry shop. Is she watching us from the window?

YOUNG STIPAN: Yes.

MISS ADAMIC: Good. Keep staring.

*(*FATHER LUKA *enters.)*

FATHER LUKA: Good day, children.

YOUNG STIPAN & MISS ADAMIC: Good day, Father.

*(*FATHER LUKA *sits.* MISS ADAMIC *curtsies and exits.)*

FATHER LUKA: Have you prepared your lesson?

YOUNG STIPAN: Yes, Father.*(He opens the book, at random, then closes it.)* No, Father, I haven't. I'm sorry.

(Beat)

FATHER LUKA: You do want to leave. Don't you.
It's all you can think about now.

YOUNG STIPAN: My mother will never let me go.

FATHER LUKA: You have been raised to be here.
How can you leave a place where people love you?
It frightens me for the country.

YOUNG STIPAN: I'm not so much good for the country.

FATHER LUKA: You are the future. Our future is going
away. No. We are selling it. We are eating our seed
corn. No. We are selling our seed corn for money to
keep our land.

YOUNG STIPAN: I would, I would send money home.

FATHER LUKA: We see plenty of money from our good
boys in America. Money that teaches us that money is
something people make somewhere else. Money that
whores us.

YOUNG STIPAN: Father?

FATHER LUKA: We will use it to buy land to starve on.
Land that has no one to work it.

YOUNG STIPAN: You could come to America too, later.
My brothers and sisters—I could save money, bring
everyone. I could work for years. I could. And bring
everyone. People do. Whole villages come, the
Amerikanac said.

FATHER LUKA: You could. I know. You could bring
the whole village to be with you in America, at great
expense. Or you could just stay here. Now, which is
more logical?

YOUNG STIPAN: But in America...everything will be different.

(IVO *enters*.)

IVO: My friend.

FATHER LUKA: Would you excuse us, please?

YOUNG STIPAN: Sir, how long does it take to bring people over? If I work hard. How long would it take before I could send for my brothers and sisters?

IVO: You could start the day you get there.

YOUNG STIPAN: How long will it take?

IVO: That depends on what other things you also decide to do.

FATHER LUKA: And your mother? Your father? Will they be coming over?

(Beat)

IVO: It's a free country. *(Off their look)* This is what people say in American when they mean, "I don't care what you do."

FATHER LUKA: They just *say* that?

IVO: *(Offhand, like an American)* "It's a free country."

FATHER LUKA: That is.... *(He is speechless.)*

IVO: They take *God's* name in vain, too, all the time. *(He kneels and scoops up a handful of earth. To* YOUNG STIPAN*)* When you come. Don't forget. Bring a little box of dirt.

YOUNG STIPAN: It will help me remember. Yes.

IVO: And if something happens, God forbid. It's good to be buried in the earth of your homeland. Or your spirit never rests. Even a pocketful. Here. *(He holds it out.)*

FATHER LUKA: Put that back. It does not belong to you. *(Beat) This* would be a free country if enough of our boys would stay in it and fight.

IVO: There are not enough boys in all Croatia to free Croatia. *(He scatters his handful of earth.)*

FATHER LUKA: You told me you came back here to die. To be buried in the earth of your homeland.

IVO: And I will be.

FATHER LUKA: But now you're going again.

IVO: And I'll come back.

FATHER LUKA: "And the Lord said to the Adversary, Where hast thou been, and the Adversary replied unto Him, I have been walking to and fro about the earth, and traveling up and down in it."

IVO: I'm not as bad as that.

FATHER LUKA: You just told this boy he could sprout his village fresh from a handful of dirt.

IVO: *(To* YOUNG STIPAN*)* He's right, it's stupid, the dirt of this place is part of you, you've already eaten enough of it. *(To* FATHER LUKA*)* Haven't we buried enough good boys here as it is?

FATHER LUKA: But if you take all our good children, who will be left? I'm supposed to be the shepherd of my little flock here. Our lambs are leaving. Soon only wolves will be left. And the weak and the old and the stupid.

IVO: And the priests. *(To* STIPAN*)* You know where to find me.

*(*IVO *goes.)*

FATHER LUKA: What does a pastor do with a congregation of wolves? A wolf bites a priest, what do you get? A holy wolf? I don't know.

YOUNG STIPAN: You could just be...

FATHER LUKA: What?

YOUNG STIPAN: Nothing, Father.

FATHER LUKA: Speak your mind, please.

YOUNG STIPAN: Maybe you could be wrong, you know, about who's staying and who's going. I want to leave for ambition, after all. To make a bigger place for myself. Maybe the wolves are the ones who are leaving.

FATHER LUKA: Only a lamb would say so. Do you think you are the only one who is too big for this place!? Stay here! Make this place bigger!

YOUNG STIPAN: How?

FATHER LUKA: Opportunity will come. I don't know when. But opportunity, sometime, must come here, our ship will come in. The Argo, maybe, a new Argo. Jason wasn't really much of a hero, you know. Not like Herakles, or Theseus, or Orpheus, Castor and Pollux. But he organized all those heroes, and more, to row together. Heroes are great men, but maybe the greatest man is the one who can gather the heroes, and organize them toward a goal. The kind of boy who dreams of making his village new in America could become that kind of man. We need that man here. You could go and discover America. But what if there is America here? Build the village new, here. Discover us.

(The bell rings.)

FATHER LUKA: Your mother is right.

YOUNG STIPAN: What.

FATHER LUKA: You see your future leaving and you learn what you want.

*(*YOUNG STIPAN *runs out.)*

(Japan, 1980s)

(JOEY sits in half-lotus position. The equipment for tea ceremony is nearby. ALMA sits with him. JOEY carefully hands her a simple teacup without a handle.)

JOEY: I hand you the cup. It rests on your palm.

ALMA: Got it.

JOEY: You turn it with the other hand.

(She does so.)

JOEY: Now. Which side is more beautiful?

ALMA: Which side of a round thing. With no ornament. Is more beautiful. This is like Catechism in Wonderland. Is this a trick question?

JOEY: Yes.

ALMA: One of those if a tree falls in the forest does it make the sound of one hand clapping deals?

JOEY: The *koans*.

ALMA: The Zen Koans. Jewish couple, Extremely Reform. *(She drinks tea.)* Oh, if Mama could see me. *(In her mother's accent)* "What is it with Americans and this picnicking? I did not come to this country so I could eat on the ground for fun. Only in America can people take a holiday to be refugees."

JOEY: She sounds like she was a funny woman.

ALMA: Ah, no. I can just imagine trying to explain to her and Papa that you've decided to grow up to be a peasant. A Japanese peasant monk.

JOEY: Imagine telling your father you grew up to be management.

ALMA: Hey, they were all that was hiring.

JOEY: I'm getting us back to our roots.

ALMA: *(In her father's accent)* Only a vegetable worries about his roots.

JOEY: Did your father say that?

ALMA: Oh, I channel him now. I'm making up new things that he would have said if he'd had the time. I catch myself thinking I must have been my parents in a past life. But since we were, after all, alive at the same time, that would suggest that since they died I've never had a soul of my own. That when they died, my soul, that girl's soul, the one I was born with... went somewhere. And my body's been carrying theirs around ever since. While mine...I don't know. It must be hanging around somewhere. May I smoke?

JOEY: You shouldn't smoke during tea ceremony.

ALMA: I'm gonna drink tea during smoking ceremony. *(She lights up.)* Okay. You like the Zen?

JOEY: I like the Zen.

ALMA: What happens when you sit there?

JOEY: I get bored and my knees hurt.

ALMA: Big change from Catholicism. This is an exercise in the exotic, you know that, right? It isn't *yours*.

JOEY: It could be.

ALMA: Nah. I've seen you play dress-up, I know what this is.

JOEY: It's an ancient system of beliefs and exercises.

ALMA: Uh huh.

JOEY: It predates Catholicism.

ALMA: Not for you it doesn't. I was with you at the font. Nothing predates Catholicism for you, young man, but labor and circumcision.

JOEY: Something else to thank you for.

ALMA: It was a status thing, okay? Didn't want you to stand in the locker room looking like a day laborer, okay? We wanted to give you all the advantages.

JOEY: Cutting off most of the means of sensation—

ALMA: Well, and it looks like you're taking care of the rest. Growing a garden out of rocks here.

JOEY: It's quiet. It flows.

ALMA: It's dead. It's a religion about trying to be dead. You used to be curious about everything, you were reading Scientific American when you were eight years old. What happened to that boy? Where did he go?

JOEY: Well, Jesus, *you* haven't been yourself since as long as I can remember.

ALMA: How long is that?

JOEY: I don't know. You used to like things better.

ALMA: Like what?

JOEY: You used to like me better.

(Beat)

ALMA: Come with me. We'll find you a Roshi wherever we go.

JOEY: You can't headhunt a Roshi.

ALMA: Wanna bet? Or we can come back.

JOEY: "Back?" This is such a bunch of... You think if you take me away somewhere, I'll forget all about this, huh.

ALMA: *Never* crossed my mind.

JOEY: "Back." Please. Where is that? You've never been *back* anywhere, Mom. Wyoming?

ALMA: Well. My parents died, honey.

(Beat)

JOEY: You lost them when you were younger than me. I can't imagine.

ALMA: Yeah. I *lost* them?

JOEY: That's how you say it.

ALMA: You make it sound like I left them behind at a rest stop. Why do you make it sound like I leave everybody?

JOEY: You left the States.

ALMA: I had *work*.

JOEY: Not everyone thinks of that as a universal blanket excuse, Mom. You left the Church.

ALMA: The Catholic Church left me high and dry.

JOEY: When you got divorced.

ALMA: I saved our lives!

JOEY: You left Dad.

ALMA: Sitting with a drink. Just sitting. *(Beat)* Dad left us, honey. He didn't mean to. He stopped being who he was.

JOEY: Nobody stays the same.

ALMA: No. But you hope you'll travel together.

JOEY: You've cut everything loose, Mom. I've seen you do it.

ALMA: Motion is relative. If I maintain a constant pace and somebody falls behind, they are doing the leaving.

JOEY: I'm not knocking it. It's very Zen.

ALMA: It is not.

JOEY: Lose all attachments. Sure. I came here, and saw this, and said, huh. A whole religion about cutting things loose. My true religion. This is the faith I was raised in. *(Beat)* Is that what happened to you?

ALMA: What.

JOEY: To make you like this.

ALMA: Like what?

JOEY: I am not the only fidgeter in the family. *You* couldn't do this.

ALMA: I could so.

JOEY: No you couldn't.

ALMA: What's the point, I don't want to be some metaphysical couch potato like you.

JOEY: Uh huh.

ALMA: What, is this a dare?

JOEY: Yeah.

ALMA: Oh well. What are we betting?

JOEY: I'll go with you.

ALMA: You'll—oh, ye of little faith. You're on, mister. One minute?

JOEY: One minute.

ALMA: Time it.

(She goes absolutely still for fifteen seconds. Then she begins weeping.)

JOEY: Mom?

(She sobs and sobs.)

(Wyoming, 1940s)

(YOUNG ALMA enters, holding the Zippo lighter. Beat)

JOSEPHINA: *(Calling, off)* Alma!

(YOUNG ALMA just sits, staring into space.)

JOSEPHINA: *(Off)* Alma! *Cara!*

(JOSEPHINA *limps in.* YOUNG ALMA *doesn't acknowledge her.*)

YOUNG ALMA: I keep waiting for a bell to ring.

JOSEPHINA: Why should there be a bell?

YOUNG ALMA: I can't believe a man is dead without the bell ringing. I keep expecting a knock at the door. Soup on the doorstep.

JOSEPHINA: You have no mouths to feed and you grieving.

YOUNG ALMA: I made your supper. Same as always.

(JOSEPHINA *sits with effort.*)

JOSEPHINA: It is hard.

(YOUNG ALMA *nods.*)

JOSEPHINA: But he was not family, Jim.

YOUNG ALMA: I liked him a lot.

JOSEPHINA: He was not a husband. Women lose husbands here.

YOUNG ALMA: An announcement at assembly. That's how I heard. Same as everybody. I don't even know how he died.

JOSEPHINA: Someone makes a stupid mistake. Like always.

YOUNG ALMA: I want to put a gold star in the window. Something.

JOSEPHINA: His mother will have a gold star in the window. You are not his poor mother.

YOUNG ALMA: No.

JOSEPHINA: Be grateful.

YOUNG ALMA: I loved him.

JOSEPHINA: Mm. Mm. But you were not—with him—
what are the *words*, ach. Do you know anything—look
at me. Do you know anything that I haven't told you?

YOUNG ALMA: About what?

(They look at each other.)

JOSEPHINA: What. What is that look.

YOUNG ALMA: I don't know.

JOSEPHINA: He was not—listen, answer me—he was not
your man, this boy?

YOUNG ALMA: What do you mean? I don't know what
you mean!

JOSEPHINA: Your body. Where does it hurt?

YOUNG ALMA: I'm tired and sad. My eyes hurt.

JOSEPHINA: Do you want your body to die?

YOUNG ALMA: What?

JOSEPHINA: Do you?

YOUNG ALMA: No... No. Why?

JOSEPHINA: You don't know what I'm talking about.

YOUNG ALMA: No.

JOSEPHINA: No. He was not your man. You are sad is
all. *Si*, okay.

YOUNG ALMA: We kissed each other.

JOSEPHINA: Mm.

YOUNG ALMA: Mama, my heart hurts.

JOSEPHINA: *Cara. Cara.* Listen, listen. You are okay.
You are.

YOUNG ALMA: It's time for your exercises.

JOSEPHINA: You don't have to, not today.

YOUNG ALMA: I'll start with your shoulders.

(YOUNG ALMA *stands behind* JOSEPHINA *and kneads her shoulders, crying silently.* JOSEPHINA *holds her hands.*)

JOSEPHINA: *Cara. Cara.* Don't be sad. You will go to college and be happy.

(Beat. YOUNG ALMA takes her hands away.)

YOUNG ALMA: But—

JOSEPHINA: We will manage.

YOUNG ALMA: But your feet.

JOSEPHINA: We will manage.

YOUNG ALMA: But your feet. The food. Your back.

JOSEPHINA: We will be okay.

YOUNG ALMA: But— *(Beat)* You will be okay.

JOSEPHINA: Yes.

YOUNG ALMA: Oh. Oh. Well. All right. I'd thought. You know. I'd been. I don't know. Helpful, but. You will be okay. Without, you know, me, so... I, uh. Yeah...

JOSEPHINA: It is time you go. Yes.

YOUNG ALMA: Yes. What have I been doing? All the things, I...spent my life indoors, my whole... These things, Jim, and Papa, you, were mine, my life. Mine. You take them, and you say —

JOSEPHINA: Yes! We will be okay! Yes! Since before you were born I take care of myself! Yes! We do not need you! Yes!

(Beat)

YOUNG ALMA: My head feels like it's been split open.

JOSEPHINA: You are all right. I seen split open. In the Great War. I seen a heart beating on the ground. You

are all right. I seen heads split open. Two times I seen
that. Gray brains. You, you are doing good, you are.

YOUNG ALMA: I don't know what to do with that
information! I can't assimilate that information out
of you right now, I can't take that in! You've been to
hell you've lived in hell, I know that much, I know
this is Heaven to you, but this is *my* hell. *Mine.*

JOSEPHINA: Not hell. This world. You do not like that
other people have been sad too, you want to be the
worst ever sad person, you who are just beginning.
You want me to tell you, do not worry you will have
as much pain as me before your life is done? You want
me to say you got more room in you than you know?
You want—I had a heartbreak, okay? Before the war,
any of the wars, before everything, all the history.
I have my heartbreak. Sitting drawing little lines in the
dust with my finger, envying the dust, heartbreak that
bad. You live in a little room, your heart, a room of
feeling, with your Mama and Papa, then this love, this
boy happens, and oh, oh, a door flies open you thought
was a closet and it is a whole 'nother room of suffering.
You walk in, live there. Dust floor. Small window. Sun
for an hour a day. Double door—what?—wardrobe or
something. Sometimes you hear a little— *(She makes a
creaking sound.)* Hinges, yes? You do not notice, too
busy suffering in your two room house. The sound
gets bigger, you look up. The doors of that wardrobe-
you-thought. History kicks those doors down like the
monster in the closet and history says right this way
and leads you out of those two little rooms of your
heartache and into a, what, a, a mansion of suffering.
Ballrooms of agony, great halls of sadness. Uniform
people, what do they—*ciceroni*, guides—lead you into
new rooms of torture, show you the treasures. You go
through, stare at the *cherubini* painted on the ceilings,
the blood on the floor, you think who? How? This is my

heart? Who could build such a palace and keep it up
and live in it? And you fall down on the stone floor,
you crawl to a corner, you see there a cornerstone, you
feel the letters carved in the stone, it says: God. And the
date is the day you were born. God built your heart for
the two of you to live. And whoever else can break in.
You want what is yours? That is yours. Is this what you
want to hear?

(Beat)

YOUNG ALMA: I should make his mother some soup.

JOSEPHINA: That is what a neighbor is for. You can see
their house from yours. You reach them if you can.

(YOUNG ALMA stands.)

YOUNG ALMA: Can I get you anything, Mama?

JOSEPHINA: Yes.

YOUNG ALMA: What.

JOSEPHINA: I am a stupid cripple woman, this language
makes me say the wrong thing. But I am watching you
for years. And I know you do not think so, living in this
gravel place, and the neighbor men dying under the
ground, and your knees bleeding from the wind in
winter, and now Jim dead. But I have seen you be
happy. Your voice when you read to me is happy. Later
maybe you remember only sadness. But you remember
this too: me telling you now. You have been happy
sometimes even here. Remember you know how.

YOUNG ALMA: I want Papa. I'm going to ask him.

JOSEPHINA: Ask him what?

(YOUNG ALMA exits.)

JOSEPHINA: *Cara bambina. Carissima bambina.*

(The lights fade.)

(Croatia, 1910)

*(*YOUNG STIPAN *sits, staring into space.* MARIJA *watches.)*

MARIJA: He told you not to go, the priest?

YOUNG STIPAN: Mm.

MARIJA: Left you to your troubles?

YOUNG STIPAN: Mm.

MARIJA: Feels bad, doesn't it.

*(*YOUNG STIPAN *nods.)*

MARIJA: Now you know how it feels.

*(*YOUNG STIPAN *nods.)*

MARIJA: You would have followed that old goat right off the edge of the world, wouldn't you, with your eyes shut and dancing the *kolo* if he'd asked you, right off the edge of the—

YOUNG STIPAN: *(Muttered)* The world is round.

MARIJA: What did you say?

YOUNG STIPAN: The world is round.

MARIJA: What about it?

YOUNG STIPAN: It's just what I said.

MARIJA: The world is round. Says who.

YOUNG STIPAN: Everybody.

MARIJA: Everybody who hasn't come to the edge of it yet.

YOUNG STIPAN: You don't believe the world is round?

MARIJA: Make me believe it and you can go.

(Beat)

YOUNG STIPAN: What?

MARIJA: You heard me.

(Beat)

YOUNG STIPAN: Would you believe the priest?

MARIJA: What does the Bible say about it?

YOUNG STIPAN: That the world is the center of the universe and everything goes around it. Sort of. But it's wrong.

MARIJA: The Bible is wrong and you're right.

YOUNG STIPAN: They couldn't see it either.

MARIJA: They?

YOUNG STIPAN: The people who wrote the Bible.

MARIJA: God wrote the Bible.

(FATHER LUKA enters.)

YOUNG STIPAN: But—

FATHER LUKA: Ma'am, Stipan, I can hear you from my study.

YOUNG STIPAN: Ask the priest. Ask him.

MARIJA: Father. What does the Church say about the shape of the world?

FATHER LUKA: Why?

MARIJA: We are confused about what to believe.

FATHER LUKA: The world is round, ma'am, the Church has been clear on this point for decades now.

YOUNG STIPAN: You see? So.

MARIJA: Where is it? In Creation. According to you.

FATHER LUKA: Well.

MARIJA: Where is the earth, Father?

YOUNG STIPAN: No!

MARIJA: What. Did you say. To me.

FATHER LUKA: We are in the public square.

MARIJA: I know where I am standing. Tell me where I'm standing. Where does the Church tell me I am standing.

FATHER LUKA: The Church has yet to reconcile its interpretation of Holy Writ with the Copernican Theory of the Solar System.

MARIJA: What does the Bible say?

FATHER LUKA: The Bible...

MARIJA: Who wrote the Bible, Father?

FATHER LUKA: Ancient patriarchs, inspired by God.

MARIJA: God wrote the Bible. God Himself. Men wrote it down. Am I right?

FATHER LUKA: Right enough.

MARIJA: Am I right?

FATHER LUKA: I will not be catechized by you, ma'am.

MARIJA: Who are you? What are you? What are you teaching my son in private? What would the bishop think of it?

FATHER LUKA: Ask him yourself. Write to him.

MARIJA: I can't.

FATHER LUKA: See him. Win him over with your charm.

MARIJA: Maybe I will. (To YOUNG STIPAN) There. Believe him now.

YOUNG STIPAN: This isn't fair!

(During the following, STIPAN enters at a distance. He stares into space.)

YOUNG STIPAN: The question was is it round, you said if I made you believe it I could go, you *said* and you asked the priest, and he says it's round, the Church says it's round, and that's all!

(The bell rings. YOUNG STIPAN *and* MARIJA *do not move.)*

MARIJA: Who the hell are you to tell me what shape the world is, like you'd know?

(The bell rings. They do not move.)

FATHER LUKA: Ma'am. Stipan.

MARIJA: *(To* YOUNG STIPAN*)* Well?

(The bell rings. They do not move.)

FATHER LUKA: You have to go. You're expected at home.

MARIJA: You think you know things because people tell you.

(The bell rings. They do not move.)

FATHER LUKA: Ma'am, Stipan, he's expecting you.

MARIJA: And you believe them, when with your own eyes you see people leave and never come back.

(The bell rings. They do not move.)

YOUNG STIPAN: They send letters. They send money.

FATHER LUKA: Stipan.

YOUNG STIPAN: Some come back.

MARIJA: From where?

YOUNG STIPAN: America.

MARIJA: They say.

YOUNG STIPAN: You think they're lying?

MARIJA: Either the world is a big ball rolling through Creation, or people lie about where they've been. Well, one I've seen for myself. Until someone I trust goes around the world and comes back here—

YOUNG STIPAN: The *Amerikanac*—

MARIJA: Someone I trust.

YOUNG STIPAN: But you wouldn't trust anybody that left here!

MARIJA: Because what kind of person does that.

YOUNG STIPAN: So how—how—

MARIJA: What how how what?

YOUNG STIPAN: How can anybody make you believe the world is round?

MARIJA: You believe anything anybody tells you! You make yourself loyal to these people, you believe anything that comes from someplace else, or a book! The more you read, the stupider you get. The less good for anything. How can you care more for something you've never seen than for what you've lived with all your life? How? This has gone long enough. Bring him back his books tomorrow. I'm stopping this.

YOUNG STIPAN: It's round!!(*He throws* MARIJA *to the ground, screaming*) I'll *show* you!!

(FATHER LUKA *rushes forward.*)

FATHER LUKA: Stipan!

(YOUNG STIPAN *puts both hands to his mouth, turns and runs away.*)

MARIJA: I'll be all right.

FATHER LUKA: Oh, madam, madam. Are you ready to stand up?

MARIJA: I have to go.

(*She waves him off and stands up on her own.*)

FATHER LUKA: Oh God save us.

MARIJA: Don't cry, Father. He'll never leave me now.

(*The lights fade.*)

(Wyoming, 1940s)

(YOUNG ALMA *enters and sees* STIPAN *waiting. She stops.*)

STIPAN: You have a question.

YOUNG ALMA: Jim's dead.

STIPAN: Yes.

YOUNG ALMA: He died because he hated what he was from.

STIPAN: Then that boy was my *paisan*.

YOUNG ALMA: Papa. You want me to leave everything. I don't even know what I'd be leaving.

STIPAN: Rock Springs, Wyoming.

YOUNG ALMA: I'd be leaving *you*. All I know about you is that you left wherever you were from. Who are you, Papa?

STIPAN: I came to this country a boy. I don't care about those people anymore.

YOUNG ALMA: What about the priest?

STIPAN: What about him?

YOUNG ALMA: The one who taught you to read. What happened to him?

(Moonlight on YOUNG STIPAN, *digging in the gravel. Surf rolls. A bundle and a bedroll are by his side.* FATHER LUKA *watches him.*)

FATHER LUKA: What are you doing?

YOUNG STIPAN: Packing.

FATHER LUKA: To go.

YOUNG STIPAN: I can't stay now.

FATHER LUKA: Saint Jerome, a learned and holy man in the fifth century, was a native of Dalmatia. One day a

man provoked him with a remark, and Jerome struck
the man, knocked him cold. Then Jerome clasped
his hands in prayer, looked heavenward, and said,
"Parce mihi, Domine, quia Dalmata sum!"

YOUNG STIPAN: I didn't learn enough Latin.

FATHER LUKA: "Forgive me, O Lord. I am Dalmatian."
You'd be forgiven.

YOUNG STIPAN: No.

FATHER LUKA: You're choosing not to be forgiven.
You're exiling yourself from grace.

YOUNG STIPAN: I'm packing for America, Father,
not for Hell.

FATHER LUKA: It's a slippery slope. Do want this?
(He holds out the book.)

YOUNG STIPAN: I couldn't take that, Father.

FATHER LUKA: Here.

YOUNG STIPAN: It's your only copy, how could you get
another, I couldn't leave you without it.

FATHER LUKA: You can take yourself away, but not the
book?

(Beat)

YOUNG STIPAN: The book isn't mine.

FATHER LUKA: It could have been.

YOUNG STIPAN: I will get a copy in America.

FATHER LUKA: Yes. I hear you can get a copy of
anything there.

(YOUNG STIPAN goes back to his digging.)

FATHER LUKA: This is in part my fault. You do not
know all of the story. Jason, at the end of his life, had

nothing. The woman who got him the Golden Fleece, whom he promised to love forever.

YOUNG STIPAN: That girl in the palace.

FATHER LUKA: Medea. He betrayed her, years later, out of ambition, and fear of her power, and she killed their children.

YOUNG STIPAN: Wait. What? She...what? Is that the end of the book?

FATHER LUKA: This is after the end of the book. Jason ended up sitting on a beach like this, leaning against the rotten hulk of the Argo, looking up at the constellations that had been his shipmates. Herakles, Castor, Pollux. Turned to golden stars, floating above him.

YOUNG STIPAN: Like the *villé*.

FATHER LUKA: No. They are too far away to care for us. They are a guide to travelers, that is all. Jason ended up sitting on a beach. Just sitting. The prow of the Argo, decayed by now, fell on his head and killed him.

YOUNG STIPAN: No.

FATHER LUKA: And Marco Polo wrote his book while he was in prison for debt. When you start as a voyager, voyaging is the only place you are at home. And the places the voyagers come from have no native sons. And a nation needs a future. It will take one from whoever offers it. We all need something that is ours. Our place. Ours. And if it's in Hell, well. It's ours. Argonauts end with nothing.

YOUNG STIPAN: A famous legend.

FATHER LUKA: Yes. A famous legend.

(YOUNG STIPAN *exits.*)

FATHER LUKA: (*Sobbing*) This poor country. This poor country.

(The lights on FATHER LUKA *fade.)*

STIPAN: The priest was stupid, for all he could read. He would go out into the countryside and get the peasants to tell him all sorts of lies about werewolves and *villés* and what all.

YOUNG ALMA: Papa? What's a *villé*?

STIPAN: Peasant ignorance. What kind of man cares more for recording ignorance than for all the truth still hidden in the world? All the discoveries. Who has time?

YOUNG ALMA: What happened to him?

STIPAN: The priest joined the *Ustache*. The Russians have probably hanged him by now.

YOUNG ALMA: What's the *Ustache*?

STIPAN: You've heard. It's been in the news.

YOUNG ALMA: They're Nazis.

STIPAN: Not Nazis.

YOUNG ALMA: They were with the Nazis. *(Beat)* That's what we're from.

STIPAN: We are not there.

YOUNG ALMA: It's what we're made of.

STIPAN: You are made of Cream of Wheat and Bosco and Log Cabin Maple Syrup. You are a girl made of science books and crystal radio kits. You are a creature that priest and those Dalmatian people could never imagine. You are against them, I made you against them.

YOUNG ALMA: What am I from if I'm not from that? Mama's people? The *Fascisti*? I wanted so much not to be from that, I thought I could be from you, your people, and it's worse!

STIPAN: Do not be from there.

YOUNG ALMA: What else can I be?

STIPAN: You are from the future. Be from the future.
Listen to me. You want to be from somewhere. Here
is where we're from. A nation with no land. Made of
its people. Every race, any region. Not loyal to our
neighbors, or a place, or a belief, but to the goal.

YOUNG ALMA: What goal?

STIPAN: *Any goal.* Learning, job, power, goodness.
Anything.

YOUNG ALMA: I don't understand.

STIPAN: You will. When you're in college. Ambition
People. Look for each other. We leave where we were
born. We find the land of opportunity. Then we're
home.

YOUNG ALMA: Papa? Are we Jews?

STIPAN: You could do a lot worse than learn from the
Jews. Never since the world began has a Jewish father
beaten his son for wanting to learn.

(Beat)

YOUNG ALMA: You left everyone you knew.

STIPAN: Yes. I did.

YOUNG ALMA: Your family.

STIPAN: Yes. I did.

YOUNG ALMA: Your Papa and Mama?

STIPAN: Yes. Yes.

YOUNG ALMA: Did you have sisters and brothers?

STIPAN: Yes.

YOUNG ALMA: I have aunts and uncles? Relatives. Papa.
I have relatives?

STIPAN: Not anymore.

(Beat)

YOUNG ALMA: They're dead?

STIPAN: I think. Yes.

YOUNG ALMA: All of them?

STIPAN: Yes.

YOUNG ALMA: Do you know for sure? Maybe—
we could find out, there might be—

STIPAN: It was an evil place. Even the priest knew.
They have been punished. There will be no one to
remember them.

YOUNG ALMA: You have to remember them.

STIPAN: I have to. Yes.

YOUNG ALMA: They couldn't all have been evil.

STIPAN: Then they are dead for sure.

YOUNG ALMA: And you left there.

STIPAN: While I had the chance. Before worse happened.

YOUNG ALMA: Worse than what? Papa? What did you
do.

(Beat)

STIPAN: I went to America. I got married. I went to
work where men go down the mines. I wait for the
men at the mouths of the holes in the earth. And when
they come out, covered in black, breathing black, I say
to them, organize. Organize. They send me to the
capitals of the country. I tell the captains of the country
there are men who spend every working day in the
underworld. I tell them we are organized. They have
tried to starve us out, they have beaten us, shot us dead
on the street. They shamed us in front of our children,
they thought we were animals, they did not think we
could think. But now they have nothing left to do to us,

and we are organized. And these captains of the country, they cannot pronounce my name, they say, what was that name again? And I say I have a new name in this country. My name is three hundred thousand votes. I fathered one child before my woman fell ill. We raised the child to be as bright as she could be. And I never laid a hand on her. I never laid a hand on another living soul again. A *villé* is a spirit killed in childhood, who travels over the world, and tries to do good.

(Beat)

YOUNG ALMA: I can't leave you.

STIPAN: You owe us nothing. The only thing a child owes her parents is the way she raises her children. You can do us no harm. No harm. Do you understand me.

YOUNG ALMA: Papa. What can I do.

STIPAN: One thing for me.

YOUNG ALMA: What?

STIPAN: I learned to think from reading books. They beat me for it. But I learned to read books. It is what I do instead of praying. So I raised you to read. Because I raised you to be the person, in the whole world, I would most admire. What you can do for me is when you travel, bring a book.

YOUNG ALMA: Papa? What's going to happen to me?

STIPAN: Here is a remarkable thing. If you keep on far enough, you will meet yourself again.

YOUNG ALMA: How?

STIPAN: If I tell you, you will not believe me. It will be a surprise. *(Beat)* Go on now.

YOUNG ALMA: Do you need anything, Papa?

STIPAN: Not anymore.

(YOUNG ALMA *walks away. Beat*)

STIPAN: How did I do?

JOSEPHINA: (*Off*) You did good, Stipan. Are you okay?

STIPAN: To stand before your child like that. Is like
standing in front of God.

JOSEPHINA: (*Off*) With God it will be easier. He is a
parent Himself.

(*The lights fade.*)

(*Japan, 1980s*)

(JOEY *is sitting* zazen, *looking out at the garden.* ALMA
enters, holding a garment bag, and stands at a distance.)

ALMA: Joey? Joe? Smidgen?

JOEY: Do you think you could please never call me that
again?

ALMA: What? Smidgen? I've always called you that.

JOEY: So?

ALMA: So. I thought I'd better tell you where I'm going.
They want me to start the ball rolling in Zagreb.

JOEY: Zagreb? It sounds like a health food cracker.
What's Zagreb?

ALMA: Zagreb is the capital of one of the Yugoslavian
states. Croatia. Where my father was from.
Communism is falling, maybe you've heard about that,
Smi—Snookums. There's oil under the Krajina and
warm-water ports on the Dalmatian coast. Plenty to
do for a people with money behind them. It's the land
of opportunity.

JOEY: *Bon voyage.*

(*Beat.* ALMA *looks out at the garden.* JOEY *looks at her.*)

ALMA: Look, we always. The family. We always said
it was for freedom, all of it, all the.... No. Opportunity.
That's all it was. It was never about freedom. It should
have been. So. My job around here, as we know, is to
lose everybody. So. I'm going to do my job now. And
you do, or not, whatever this is. Or not.

JOEY: And not.

ALMA: Don't joke with me. You've never lost a child,
I'm losing a child so don't make jokes.

JOEY: Okay.

ALMA: Anyway, you do whatever... God damn it.
Trying to give you my blessing, like all the parents.
It's a curse. Never mind. Good bye. *(She turns away.)*

JOEY: Here.

ALMA: What.

*(JOEY pulls out something gift-wrapped in a cloth, Japanese-
style.)*

JOEY: This is yours.

(She takes it.)

JOEY: For the trip.

*(She opens the wrapping. It is an old book. She runs her hand
down the spine. She recites from memory.)*

ALMA: "You don't know about me. Without you have
read a book. By the name of *The Adventures of Tom
Sawyer*. But that ain't no matter." Remember when
I read you this whole book over the phone? Did the
best job I could, kiddo. Whole book. Remember?

(JOEY thinks for a moment.)

JOEY: "But I reckon I got to light out for the territory
ahead of the rest. Because Aunt Sally she's going to

adopt me and sivilize me. And I can't stand it. I been there before. The End. Yours truly. Huck Finn."

ALMA: Amen. *(Beat)* My Papa was right.

JOEY: What do you mean?

ALMA: If I tell you, you will not believe me. It will be a surprise. *(She wipes her eyes.)* I know the customs, I should give you something, too.

JOEY: Nah.

(She takes out her Zippo lighter and holds it out to him.)

ALMA: Here.

JOEY: I should start smoking?

ALMA: It's not just for that. Like this. *(She lights it and looks at the flame.)* It's for remembering with.

JOEY: Remembering what?

(She hands him the lighter.)

ALMA: "Remember, O monks, that all this world is on fire."

(Beat)

JOEY: You remembered that.

ALMA: Of course I remember it. You read it to me.

(In the distance, the others are entering, dressed for journeys, carrying their baggage: EUGENE, YOUNG STIPAN, STIPAN, JOSEPHINA, Y OUNG ALMA.*)*

*(*ALMA *turns, picks up her luggage, and heads up to join the other travelers.* JOEY *sits, holding the flame. He lifts it at arm's length, looking at it, and through it at the world.)*

END OF PLAY

www.ingramcontent.com/pod-product-compliance
Lightning Source LLC
Chambersburg PA
CBHW052149090426
42741CB00010B/2202